MAD DOG KILLERS

THE STORY OF A CONGO MERCENARY

Ivan Smith

Helion & Company Ltd

30° South Publishers (Pty) Ltd

Co-published in 2012 by:

Helion & Company Limited
26 Willow Road
Solihull
West Midlands
B91 1UE
England
Tel. 0121 705 3393
Fax 0121 711 4075
email: info@helion.co.uk
website: www.helion.co.uk

and

30° South Publishers (Pty) Ltd.
16 Ivy Road
Pinetown 3610
South Africa
email: info@30degreessouth.co.za
website: www.30degreessouth.co.za

Designed and typeset by Farr out Publications, Wokingham, Berkshire, England
Cover design by 30° South Publishers (Pty) Ltd., South Africa
Printed in the UK by Lightning Source, Milton Keynes, Buckinghamshire, and in South
Africa by Pinetown Printers (Pty) Ltd, Pinetown, KwaZulu-Natal

Text copyright © Ivan Smith 2012
Photographs as individually credited

ISBN 978-1-920143-51-0 (South Africa)
ISBN 978-1-907677-78-6 (UK)

British Library Cataloguing-in-Publication Data
A catalogue record for this book is available from the British Library

Contents

List of Illustrations

Introduction

This memoire is a record of a personal experience in the Congo as a volunteer in the *Armée Nationale Congolaise* as a mercenary. It is a brief record of a few months in the life of a young and cocky youth who believed he was afraid of nothing, but soon learnt all about fear. All young men are fearless until they meet death measuring them up close. Fear came early in the six-month contract, and overstayed its welcome. What my fellow mercenaries saw, and felt, can only be guessed at so is not touched on in this memoire. When guns are being fired in anger detailed memory suffers, as the mind is fully occupied with more immediate things than remembering, so some detail is missing.

The events of that summer of 1964 still haunt my waking dreams today. In the crowded, electronic modern world the events described will seem abnormal, not everyday happenings and certainly not in the general experience of ordinary men today. Life as a combat soldier is increasingly remote from the ken of most, certainly in those countries where there is any law and order. In remote times like those of the Roman Caesars', say, almost all men had firsthand experience of war. Today, war, when it occurs, is short lived and is fought by a minute section of the population and normal citizens have only a slight idea of the reality of war. Killing other men is no longer in the ambit of normal, civilized life.

Mercenary. There is a lot of myth and legend clouding the concept of a mercenary. In most men there is an underlying basic instinct to hunt and kill, but in today's city life that instinct has been deeply suppressed. Some fortunate are able to arrange to hunt animals but very few hire themselves out to hunt man, the ultimate prey. My own transformation from farm boy to a bloody-handed hired soldier came about courtesy of the environment and times I was born to. Central Africa some sixty years ago was not the same as today. All living things are shaped by the environment into which they emerge and that environment changes yearly. But the essential, basic core of man never changes; the inner flame does not interact with time and circumstance, does not age like the body or mind. The inner flame is not of this world and is untouched by the elements.

That long ago summer I and my companions were nominally soldiers but there is little mention of tactics, campaigns and deployments. Of conventional warfare there was none; 5 Commando Group was nominally a military unit, but military order was very lax or totally missing. Loyalty to country or unit did not exist. With no loyalty to the unit and fear of death the only commander, it was necessary to have a few close friends for mutual support. That small group was where the only loyalty lay, each caring for the life of his mates as though they were also his own insurance. Many were shot by fellow soldiers, usually in drunken arguments. I was present at some of these incidents and heard about others. Some were killed by fellow soldiers during a firefight with the enemy; a bullet in the back during a firefight solicited no questions. The only law was the small, tight-knit group. During the six months contract I served, more mercenaries died by the hand of fellow soldiers, or in misfortunes such as accidental discharges, than were killed in action against the Simba rebels.

The reader will find very little about the politics of the Congo at that time. The situation in that troubled country changed almost weekly. Even today the rule of the warlord remains in most of the Congo. There was no blanket cover by news media in those few short days to keep us informed of the political events in the country. The only news we got in the field came over the 'bush telegraph' and normally only long after an event happened. The mercenaries could not 'read' the ever-present talking drums which were the local equivalent of news media, and so, were in the dark while the local tribesmen knew the latest news. Except for a brief time under colonialism, the law in Africa has always been the law of the strong. The man who commands the strongest army is the ruler; what the strongest man decrees is the law. The self established ruler owns the country and all in it. The Congo had a few brief years of experimental democracy after the Belgians left. It did not take long before warlords rose, as they flourish where there is little infrastructure and order, and where there is no central government it is tribe versus tribe.

Early in the independence from Belgium Mobutu took total control of the army; the only faction armed with modern weapons was that army, and Mobutu soon made himself president for life. For four or more decades he looted the country whose resources he treated as his own, just as King Leopold of Belgium had. The Congo was their personal property. Mobutu kept a tight grip into old age when he was overthrown by Kabila (senior), a warlord from the north, with the help of Ugandan fighters. Kabila was murdered in a palace *coup*; his son took over. To this day intermittent rebellion simmers, and big areas are controlled by brutal warlords and their rapacious gangs. The Congo is a vast country and has virtually no infrastructure; what roads there once were are mostly gone. The Government has control in the bigger cities, which are fast crumbling. In the forest oceans tribal chiefs reign and go to war as they have done for centuries. The state of ninety per cent of the country is as it was found by Europeans two hundred years ago. Recent media reports say between 2005 and 2011, 200,000 have been killed and 20,000 people are raped each year in intermittent warfare in the Congo.

By 1964 the country had been under black rule for only three or four years, but already the infrastructure everywhere was collapsing. The railways had stopped running, the tarred roads were so rutted as to be unusable and the dirt roads were almost impassable; the only hospitals that still had doctors or medicines were those run by missionaries. The towns showed all the signs of slow decay; mountains of uncollected household rubbish, houses in once well-off suburbs looted and skeletal. There are very few cities anywhere in Africa where the buildings have been maintained in any way since the hated whites left. The African decay which covers most of the continent goes back to the 1950s' winds of change but in some older cities, such as Mombasa, the decay goes back many more years to the days when the Arabs and other alien rulers left.

Although time has dimmed the names and faces of those who were there, men with me have deliberately not been fully identified. The few who remain, or relatives of those not of this earth, may not want identification, or to be reminded of some of the things relatives were responsible for. My hope and belief is those mentioned and partially identified will not have objections. The names of them, and others, do not matter. The events were orchestrated by time and circumstance and were not extraordinary in days gone by, but would certainly cause offence in the more gentle modern world.

That strange and savage interlude taught me lot about the side of life normally hidden from men. In the tropical forest of the Congo my youthfully presumed immortality vanished and was replaced by an understanding of man's inhumanity. The cruelty innate in man is drawn from a deep, bitter and unending well. Another lesson quickly learnt was that men are fragile and die very easily, contrary to what most young men believe. Death makes the body ugly, and it is not just the ugliness of physical damage to the body by application of force, but the ugliness of a body once the spirit has left it. A body without a spirit in it becomes nothing but a part of the earth like wet mud; with the spirit still living it is not of the earth and has some beauty. Those who have killed know this.

The lust for killing permeates Africa. Another enduring lesson learnt; one that cannot be forgotten by anyone living in Africa. There are many African countries today in which rival groups constantly attack and kill each other. The war in Sudan goes back a couple of centuries. Today in many of the Central African countries warlords are carving out empires. The normal daily routine in some African countries is rape and murder by the armies of the warlords. The press sometimes report these atrocities but the rest of the world shrugs. What do you expect in Africa?

It is not only in the jungles of Central Africa or the Sahel that killing and looting flourish. Since black government came to South Africa in the early 1990s there have been over 12,000 attacks on white farms by armed black gangs. As of May 2010, 3,365 white farmers and members of their families have been murdered in these attacks, some of them in circumstances of brutality to rival any massacre in the

Congo. Farmers continue to be murdered in their homes at the rate of about one a week. More whites have been killed by marauding blacks in South Africa in the last 15 years than the total of whites murdered in the last sixty years in Kenya, Congo, Katanga and Rhodesia.

In any other continent except Africa these killings would provoke a national emergency. Imagine the outcry in Italy, Japan or Denmark if five commercial farmers were murdered by armed gangs. Imagine the outcry if that was the murder tally month after month. The United Nations has a complaint of genocide laid before it by a South African right wing political party but shows not the slightest interest. What do you expect in Africa? The killing is described by the South African government as normal criminal activity, not politically motivated. The irony here is that in Africa politically motivated murder is acceptable and in some places an everyday event. Criminal murder is just one of those unfortunate things.

1

On the south-east coast at the bottom end of Africa, inland from what is known as the Garden Route in the Republic of South Africa, is the rural village of Joubertina. It stands in a valley that runs for over a hundred kilometres between the mountains that rim the ocean to the south and the mountains that rise in serried ranks to the north. It is about 20 kilometres from the sea; very far south in Africa. I retired to this village by chance, but as the clock turns Africa back to medieval times I am glad to be far so from it all.

An extended family from the fruit lands of Germany travelled in a wagon train heading towards the East Cape in the early 1800s. They were skilled in fruit growing, knew about peaches, plums, apples and pears; fruit that needs cold winters and water to irrigate the orchards. The Kritzinger families were on the way north on the old inland wagon trail that avoided the deep river gorges along the coast. They saw the valley, approved and stayed. The chosen place is semi-desert, where the endless mountain flanks are bare of trees. Black-stemmed aloes and shrubs grow on the stony hillsides, and small tufts of tough grass. It is cold and rainy in winter so ideal for apples and other pomes fruit.

A prevailing east wind often blows off the sea and picks up moisture which drops as rain as it crosses the mountains to the south of the valley. From these southerly, seaboard mountains run streams of crystal clear water, and along which bracken and heather grow at higher altitude and then as they gurgle down the lower valley lush reeds and grass line the rivulets. The German family knew the value of the desert land with available water and founded the village and planted orchards. Those orchards now spread through the long valley and in this 21st century those who live in the valley still depend on the fruit industry. The fruit farms and the pack stores give work to most residents. Some families have worked the fruit farms for generations and are of mixed race, with German and Bushman antecedents. Those two races were the only humans living in the semi-desert for many decades. The fruit industry supports only a sparse population and in the village called Joubertina a few merchants' buildings are scattered along the one town road.

Traffic on the main highway that runs along the mountainside above the village is light. The sounds of cattle calling, tractors working, geese fighting in the sky and distance dogs barking substitute for the roar of big city traffic. In the new century, the year 2000, I came here to live in rural quiet after the sprawl and smog of Cape Town after sixteen years with the security department at the University of Cape Town. The proceeds of selling my house in the pretty little west coast suburb of Flamingo Vlei bought a rambling, broken-down, thatched farmhouse with ramshackle outbuildings on a hectare of land in the southern slopes above the village, the slopes opposite to where the main road runs and outside the municipal boundary. My early years were spent on my grandfather's farm in the midlands of what was then Rhodesia. The family were poor and lived in hard circumstances and so I am comfortably at home here in the long fruit valley in an old farmhouse. Some of my family live nearby.

An old friend, Armand, lives in a mobile home and recently drove it from a wet summer in Scotland down to Derbyshire where it was warmer and drier. He does not like England's weather. He is a man of Africa and once we were stationed together in the remote Zambezi Escarpment. We drank a lot and seduced a lot of women and sometimes attended to our police duties. He doesn't like England either and roams the continent of Europe a lot. He tried Bermuda or one of those places, maybe Jamaica, once, but found a Caribbean paradise too close, in all respects, to black Africa. He sometimes phones me, and we talk of distant days in that Shangri-La that was the country of my birth, Rhodesia, and to where my soul yeans to return. The country Mugabe has ground down until today is the poorest, worst-run country in the world, but still the African rulers give him standing ovations when he struts at their comic talk-shops and forums.

"I have just the thing for you," Armand says, talking loudly on his cell phone while sitting in some English summer field. He is excited. He always is. "You should write a book about mercenaries."

"How did you come to that conclusion?"

"You were a Congo mercenary."

Funny how he always adds 'Congo' to 'mercenary' believing it gives an added touch of menace to the word. Funny that thing about mercenaries giving a tingle of dread, because mercenary is what most professional soldiers are. All soldiers in peacetime are motivated by money, even those who say they are in it to serve the country. Very few western armies do not employ men from other lands. Surely if you are not a native of the land in whose army you serve you are a mercenary? The British army has many South Africans, Indians and others from ex- colonial lands in it. The Americans in Iraq have thousand of paid foreign staff. So the question is why does 'Congo mercenary' cause such interest in others? Maybe the media built a bogeyman; or maybe the Congo really is the heart of darkness. Those who have been there, even for a few days, will know if the description is valid. Certainly the hot fetid jungles of the Congo have refined the practice of cruelty of man to man.

"That was a hell of a long time ago, Armand. And I was there only for a short time."

That conversation was forgotten until a visit to the bank which is across the road from the now disused railway station where a crumbling, vandalized steam engine stands next to the deserted station. Once again the septic tank was spilling sewerage down the main road, so my truck had to be parked on the uphill side of the bank. It was necessary to walk on the north side broken pavement so as not to soil my shoes. Crossing the road a thought came to me. Was the Congo of 1964 catching up with me again? That long-ago decaying chaos is mostly forgotten. Had it come down to the most southern tip of Africa? Maybe it was time to revisit a short spell of life that once had a major influence on me. Maybe putting it down on paper will allow me to see the situation here in a different light.

As the biblical age touted as the end of life is reached, all around are echoes from the Congo of 1964. Those in power display rampant greed and no day goes by without some corrupt official being exposed by the media. Looting, be it graft by the elected politicians, or by large gangs of heavily armed men rampaging through shopping malls, or battering cash-in-transit vans off the road, is rampant. Unlike in the Congo there is still some law and order. It seems to me looting is the trademark of Africa. Power and phones lines are stolen on a regular basis; even railway tracks are uprooted and sold. Here sometimes there are arrests, unlike the Congo, but for how much longer law and order will be enforced is uncertain, as time and again politicians breaking the laws are ignored by enforcers. In Africa the law does not apply to ruling politicians.

In the days of Shaka, and other Africa kings, anyone who had better crops or cattle than a neighbour was pointed out as a witch and impaled in the cattle kraal and his possessions were then shared between the ruler and his accusers. In modern Africa things have not changed much. In Africa people are still being identified as witches and killed and their possessions looted. Nearly every month the South African press reports such cases; normally well-off and elderly people in rural areas are pointed out and stoned. There are also regular ritual murders reported where body parts are harvested for black magic. Such conduct would make world headlines if it happened in the West. Witches? So what, it is only Africa! Of course, In South Africa the whites are all witches; in the rest of Africa anyone with assets is.

The decay in the village brings to me a feeling of inevitable, impending doom. Most of my life was spent fighting to keep my country, Rhodesia, out of black hands. Failure to do so destroyed hundreds of thousands of lives. While with the British South Africa Police my service included spells with the paramilitary Support Unit, and the Police Anti-Terrorist Unit, both dedicated to fighting terrorism. Rhodesia is no more. Zimbabwe is also no more, the mass murderer and master looter Mugabe has totally decimated it by his greed. Now South Africa, the country of my ancestors is beginning to show all the symptoms of rule by black despots. I hope my dread is but prejudice.

These then are the paths that lead to the primordial forests of the Congo where butterflies do duty as vultures.

Violence came into my life at a very young age. At junior school one childish game was trying to recall earliest memory, trying to remember the earliest days. I regressed in my mind back as far as possible. There was a dew-wet fallow maize field filled with spear grass and the early morning sun made diamonds of the dewdrops stuck on the spiderwebs. It was cold and I was wearing a bib and a pair of dungarees. My brother, who is three years older than me, was aiming the .22 rifle at a dove cooing in nearby tree. I must have been about four years old. Did we eat that dove? That early image stuck in my mind so today the details can still be recalled, but I fixed only the image of me in the dew-wet field. If the dove was shot it would have been eaten; using guns and killing began very, very early on.

My father's family emigrated from England to South Africa in the 1820s and established a farm where they introduced chicory and grew rich in the little East Cape village of Alexander. My paternal grandfather and his four sons moved to Rhodesia before the Second World War, and founded another farming dynasty there. My mother's family were Afrikaans farmers who moved to Rhodesia in the early founding years of that country, in the late 1800s. As a child I spoke only Afrikaans and Shona, first learning English at school. The early days were spent on a farm in the midlands of Rhodesia, where the house was built of thatched poles and mud walls and there was no running water, telephone or electricity.

There is another early childhood memory of running down the steps of the old tin and thatch homestead, which was built under tall blue gums to look up at the sky at thunder passing overhead and the metallic grey shape of a massive four-engined bomber. There was shouting and excitement as the bomber roared overhead and then vanished behind the ridge where the neighbours lived, about five kilometres away. Soon there was the sound of metal tearing and then a rumbling, a booming earth-shaking explosion and in the distance behind the far ridge a tall column of black smoke mushroomed skywards. That must have been at about the same time as my earlier memory. I was born in 1941 and that crashed airplane was on a practice flight from Gwelo airfield laden with training bombs. World War Two was still ongoing. How did I know it was an aircraft? It must have been the first one I ever saw, that big old war bird. Maybe someone told me what it was afterwards. A monument was built to the dead, a propeller from the bomber mounted on a plinth in the mealie field where it fell. We visited the crash site and the field smelt of blood and gunpowder; the smell of death. That familiar smell has been with me often over the years.

We grew up wild and untamed, barefoot and hunting the animals in the veldt with catapult, sling, bow and gun. When the school insisted shoes had to be worn it was with reluctance that I complied. The farm home was left behind for boarding school at the age of ten. By that age guns and death were familiar and I could be trusted to shoot an ox and then skin, gut it and process the meat for the house. I knew very well what a gun was for. Death was familiar and death fed the family. Predators do not pity food. Much later I learnt of the other, very different death: that of man. Progress from hunter to trained man-killer was also at a young age.

Boarding school was government subsidized and so children of the poor went to boarding school. We travelled by train from Salisbury to Que Que, a steam train which took all day to do the 150 kilometres, and we arrived smelling of coal. Once on the way to school my elder brother wanted the top bunk, but I beat him to it so he yanked me off by my leg. The steel ashtray that folded out from the cabin wall on a bottom swivel gouged my thigh as I fell and a chunk of meat ended up in the ash -tray. When punched on the nose he did nothing because he was feeling guilty. That day I first felt the power and freedom of being strong and self-reliant. That scar on my thigh is still there sixty years on and always reminds me not to fear other men.

After final exams I never once returned to visit that high school where I learnt about girls and not much else. The strongest memory of high school is awakening sexual desire. Because of girls my shoes were regularly worn and my hair combed. The rules and regulations and studying and learning were hated intrusions. I was no good at any of it; it interfered with freedom and independence too much

There is part of me, a part that never leaves, that yearns for those youthful days and the freedom of the open veldt and the limitless horizon, the yellow moon rising over a stark baobab tree, a flooded river thundering rain-swollen between banks. No other man's rules to tie me down. Jump into the flooded river and let the current go where it would and paddle only hard enough to keep the head above water. I wandered the vast, wild area of the family farm in school holidays, staying out for days, sleeping in caves and eating doves and wild fruit. At boarding school I wanted that back, and that is still where my soul still lives. I am a child of the African veldt and would be as untamed as any bush animal if given the choice. But today the animals are gone from the forests of Africa, and the forests themselves are going to the charcoal ovens and I am caged by convention like most modern city-living men are.

Elvis Presley, rock and roll, stove-pipe jeans, leather jacket and hair slicked back with Brylcreem. Every night jiving and seeking the woman who might say yes, fighting and being cool. My mother was already in despair and worried about my future. I was staying at home and so had to take heed of her concerns. She booked me into the University of Cape Town on a bursary from the State Lottery as the son of a war veteran. My father had been with the Ghurkhas during the Second World War in Burma and India. That meant the British Government, who then ruled Rhodesia, would sponsor my education. Would my life have turned out different with university education or had Britain not thrown Rhodesia to the wolves? The future and past are not reachable.

The winds of change began blowing but were not heard because none of us colonialists were listening. While waiting to go to university, my mate Errol drove down the road in an Austin Healy 300/6. His hair was slicked back and he wore white-rimmed dark glasses. His big six cylinder, shark-bonneted, open sports car growled and burbled as he waved. Right then, more than anything that big, long sports car and lots of money and all that went with it became all that mattered. With only that a man could pick and choose the girls; they would queue up. The Healy and money was the answer to the good life. An education was nothing, money was all. That same lust drove me for many years after leaving school.

At the time I was working as an assessor in the Tax Department. My need for a job, and a notice of vacancies on a pin-board in the post office, coincided. The job consisted of sitting in an office looking at forms all day. The Tax Department was in a big building and so there were lots of young woman to keep me interested and sane for a while. Life was then music, booze and girls. The salary was £360 a year, £30 a month. That bought a bicycle to get to work, back for lunch and then home again at 4.30pm. Affording a bicycle was considered lucky; many could only afford the bus. Those with who have nothing are always satisfied with little.

Physical fitness is something that is essential for a long, enjoyable life. Fitness was part of my life and has always been so; ten miles each way, 40 miles a day on the bicycle. The previous year I had been captain of the rugby, water polo and gymnastics teams at school and also cricket and boxing. Forty miles a day on a bicycle was nothing. By the age of twelve my body was already fully grown to six foot two and 200lbs: working as hard as a grown man on the farm made sure of that. Club rugby and swimming remained a passion after school. Playing sport to stay fit gave way to other things, but a morning run was a lifetime habit. At a rock and roll session we talked, Errol and me, and he told me how to get that Healy Six. A job on the Copper Belt on the Northern Rhodesian mines was the answer to the Holy Grail.

The year 1959 found me as an eighteen-year old and signed on as a miner at the lowest legal age. Lonrho mining company signed me up at the fancy multi-storied building in Salisbury with waterfalls in the foyer. Starting wages as a learner official would be £150 month, plus a hundred underground danger pay and a monthly copper bonus then running at 75 per cent of salary, £430 a month; that was more than a year's pay at the tax department. That money broke my mother's heart. Money blinds the poor very easily. The Healy came out of the first month's salary with change to spare. What else does a randy, strong eighteen-year-old youth need out of life but money and a fancy sports car? Mining underground? Dangerous work? When you are young and strong and quick and alive, danger is only an added excitement and enjoyment.

The copper mine was in the village of Mufulira. It is near the Congo border, near the Katanga Province and city of Elizabethville where there were diamond mines and other rich minerals. That city was a small Paris in those days of Belgian rule. Diamond smugglers came across the border and often at night in the mine single-quarters a black man would knock on the door and offer a stone. There was extreme danger of arrest in this, as one never knew if the man was a police informer and the detectives were hiding round the corner waiting for the buy to be made. It was a time to make a quick and right decision, or spend years behind bars. I bought a couple of times taking the risk, but the next step was selling and the only buyer was the Greek who owned the general dealer's shop in the main street of the small town and the price was set so low it was not worth it.

It was those diamonds in Katanga and the other mineral wealth including copper that fixed in mind a picture of a country with endless wealth, of gold and diamonds that could be picked up off the ground, wealth there for the taking. The truth is Katanga is nearly like that nirvana of imagination and the mines have been, and still are, looted by a variety of despots. Various armies and warlords have been running the Katanga mines for many decades now. Mugabe sent in his army with his handpicked generals to support the elder Kabila and for many years those generals looted and shared the riches with Mugabe. The Congo President, the younger Kabila, is today still too weak to do anything about the exploitation of the Katanga wealth.

On Copper Belt mines, as in all mines, danger is part of the deal. It is not possible for a man to extract wealth from deep in the earth without being in extreme danger. When there are millions of tons of rock above the crawl hole, and there is no way of stopping that rock collapsing, only delaying it long enough to get the ore out, then life is at risk. On the Copper Belt the weight of the overhang was not the only danger. There was also plenty of underground water. The area is sub-tropical with heavy annual rain and that rain does not all run off in rivers; a great deal of it is stored in aquifers underground. On the copper mines teams go in to drain the underground lakes ahead of development. The drainage teams go down the drive to the face and a steel door with pipes and air valves is closed behind the team. They blast and smash rock until the drive is five metres from the lake and then put in charges a last time and come out and shut the door. If all is well the charge breaks the rock bulkhead and releases the lake and the water floods to the steel door from where it is piped to surface. Most of the Northern Rhodesian mining town's water supply came from those underground lakes.

Sometimes the underground water goes undetected and a development driveway hits an area where the rock is so waterlogged it has turned to mud. As the drill crews hammer the bulkhead drilling holes to put charges in, the rock face suddenly melts and millions of tons of sodden rock, a wall of mud, rushes down the drive. Then a mudslide avalanche sweeps the underground railways away and minces the puny bodies of miners. But danger brings with it very high rewards and those who survive live very well, well enough to lure recruits to fill the shoes of the dead. That mining environment was also one that shaped me, an environment where danger and fear, in myself, and in my fellow men, was always present and familiar. Man learns from all the passing show of life, the good and the bad.

When a man goes underground in a deep mine he must control fear. To work in a mine a man must steel his heart and body to fear. When there is no light but the lamp on the helmet, where if the artificial light goes out a hand touching your face cannot be seen, then you block off fear of the dark. When you stand at the top of a black hole going down solid jagged rock hundreds of feet and you climb down that black hole on a vertical steel ladder whose steel rail steps are backed by wooden boards so gumboots do not slip through the rungs, and the hand rails are wet with condensation, then you put your fear of heights away. When you get into the man cage that takes you into the black from surface, a cage the size of a railway carriage standing on its head, and there are two hundred other men in the cage, so the cable stretches a metre, and the winding engine driver thinks it is a joke to let the cage drop in freefall so your feet come off the ground and you float, then you put aside vertigo.

Thursday evenings were the worst time to ride the man hoist. Thursday was the evening when visitors were allowed to ride the man cage and visit the better, safer parts of the mine, safer being relative. That was the night the visitors, men and women dressed in clean blue overalls and wearing white helmets like shift bosses, and clean gum boots, gathered nervously at the man hoist cage. If you were going on shift then you braced yourself for the worst as the cage man closed the doors and rang his signal to the winding engine driver. As the cage carried only a dozen or so people, and not the hundreds it carried at a shift change, the hoist driver had lots of scope to play and he used it to the full, throwing the big drums into free spool and keeping it that way until a few metres from the level where you got out. Then he would gently apply brakes to stop the freefall, and follow with a hard stop so the cage bounced on the cable, the sill rising and falling in the doorway. The stifled screams of the visitors amused the cage man. The fear of others is funny.

The danger on the Copper Belt did not only come from the bowels of the earth. The men who mined were as hard as the rock they fought underground. Climbing hundreds of metres up and down each shift made men hard, lifting rock made them hard, pushing explosive charges into holes with wood stakes, so as not to ignite the charge early, made them hard. Working with pneumatic rock drills that created a sound so loud it could not be heard but only felt in the air as a vibration, made them deaf and deaf men are loud and rambunctious. There was danger in all the social events of the mining town, danger from hard, loud and strong men, addicted to the feel of danger, who sought the danger as a drug. That too was the environment that shaped me.

A fresh eighteen-and-a-bit-year old lad was bait to the older miners, a chicken to pluck. It did not matter that I was large and very fit and had done a lot of boxing; it was better not go to the Mufulira Hotel bar on a Friday or Saturday night. Once on my own had been enough; the lesson had been learnt and the mine recreation club was my choice. Then Ron came into my life. He was a large, raw-boned Afrikaner who shared the single-quarter with me. The accommodation was a four-roomed house, two rooms each side with a gauzed-in veranda each and a shared bathroom and toilet at the back. The rooms were not inter-leading so one could ignore the housemate if you chose to. Ron was not someone easily ignored. He had a bad stutter and a wart on his penis. His face was covered in scars, his eyebrows white welts, and part of an ear was missing; the other one also showed tooth marks. Ron wanted me to go with him when he picked his regular fight on Friday and Saturday night. Fighting was his favourite entertainment, and he needed me to go with him because the brawlers in the bar had learnt not to pick on him. Ron could pick his fight when the rock-breakers baited me, his friend.

Every weekend at closing time the rock-breakers milled around loudly abusing each other, trying to provoke a fight and inevitably a tough miner would grab my shirt front and stick his face against mine and enquire if I wanted to make something of it. Ron would push the man back and say he would make something of it, and took the other by the throat with his left hand. Punches would rain on Ron's head and face. Ron's right hand would clench and cock back behind his shoulder, the whole time his left throttling the punching man, and then the right would thunder against the man's face and Ron opened his left hand and the miner fell unconscious on the floor. This was repeated many times over the months.

How times have changed. There was never any police involvement in those days when fighting was regarded as a legitimate sport. There was no animosity afterwards, no civil suits or charges of assault laid. Maybe there would be less violent crime today if men were still allowed to indulge in physical fighting. How did it come about that all such pursuits are so stigmatized in most of the world today? Has society become too ruled by its feminine side? A certain yearning to return to those wild, manly days comes back when dreaming in the sun.

Those sessions taught the value of having a strong man on your side. Physical fighting and learning to control other men is a very valuable thing to any would-be soldier. It came to me gradually in my life as part of the environment into which I was born. That life is passed. The warriors of old, who fought with sword and club were the last men to earn the right to be called warriors. Those who were the most fearless were the most highly regarded. Is being fearless no longer needed in today's soft world? Possibly not, as today cowards can kill just as effectively as a fearless man. Today's weapons allow a man to kill from afar and stay remote from the act of killing. Maybe if wars were still fought hand to hand, and those who declared war were required to lead from the front, there would be a lot less war.

Those Copper Belt days were lived out near the border of the Katanga Province of the Congo. There was no way of seeing the future that would take me to that country. Politics was very far from my interests; I knew nothing of what was happening in my own land, knew even less about what went on in other parts of the world. The newspapers and media played a very small role in my life and in society in general then. News media had not penetrated all aspects of living as it has done today. Television was introduced to the country while I was mining; what concerned politicians seemed comical posturing at the time. The hand of government was still very light in those days; the free-spirited citizens of the Federation made sure the politicians did not interfere too much. The all-powerful centralized state did not exist in The Federation of Rhodesia and Nyasaland.

A constant in all British territories was once the need for a standing army. The belief throughout the Commonwealth was that one day there would be another major war and British subjects would be called to the defence of Britain. The use of young men as cannon fodder is an old and widespread practice. At the age of twelve I had been drafted into the school cadets and we wore the badges of Britain. The headmaster, who was also the hostel housemaster, ordered me to report to the parade square next to the armoury. A .303 Lee Enfield Mk 1V was put in my hands. I was ordered to march and fix bayonet and squeeze off aimed shots on the range at Bisley targets out to 500 yards. After range work boiling water was poured down the barrels of the old rifles to clean them, a practice which dated from black-powder days. Rhodesia was a British colony and a Rhodesian saluted the Union Jack. No-one asked my thoughts on that, only "fall in, and quick march". So from an early age I was a soldier under command of those who were British through and through. Discipline instilled by British army training is hard to shake off.

Within months of leaving school the call-up to Territorial training arrived. For six months my body and soul belonged to the staff at the Heany Barracks outside Bulawayo. Each day was long and extremely physically testing. Hours of marching and running and nights spent digging trenches. Every waking second under the command of vicious corporals and sergeants with loud voices, who delighted in pushing men to exhaustion and beyond as any dissent meant weeks in detention barracks. My added burden was being made a Bren gunner; the machine gun was twice as heavy as a rifle and a lot more difficult to carry comfortably. On 'battle practice' riflemen were issued with blanks to fire, the Bren number two, who carried twenty empty spare magazines, had a wooden football rattle with which to simulate machine gun fire. The culmination of all the marching was the pass-out parade. The company like robots polished and shiny, cleated boots like a cannon shots on the tar, one loud sound in unison. For many weeks after leaving the barracks my body would jerk to attention at any loud voice.

Our training was that laid down by the British Army over the centuries. The orders given while marching and doing arms drill were those from hundreds of years ago. The arms and equipment all dated from the Second World War or before. The webbing was that of a British soldier from the First World War, the ammunition pouches each side of the chest on web straps that ran over the shoulders, linked to the belt front and back. Canvas small and big packs clipped onto the same straps at the back, and a greatcoat of felt made up full battle order. The black leather boots were iron-studded. Puttees wrapped the ankles. It was all outdated, uncomfortable and impractical. The strict discipline was hammered into all recruits. Recruits were allowed to saying only one thing; "Yes. SIR."

As a Territorial, one had to serve the army for many years and give a weekend a month to training. The assumption was always that you were a willing participant in the military. When the state needed to activate an army in any emergency, a Territorial had to heed the call. It is said that army service teaches a boy discipline. Maybe it does, but it also makes a boy yearn to put all military matters behind him and get on with living. That it did to me.

In the Federation of Rhodesia and Nyasaland the early 1960s was when the Black Nationalist movement began to agitate for black rule and the murders which plagued the region for twenty years began. The Territorials of the Northern Rhodesia Regiment were called up and spent endless days in the Kitwe mine sports club hall waiting for the police to call them to assist in quelling the riots. That call never came. While lolling around in the sports hall, where blanket rolls were spread on the hard, wooden floor, radios provided some distraction. It was radio news that informed us the Belgian Government had suddenly caved in and had handed the Congo, whose border was nearby, over to the blacks. That news was incredible and almost unbelievable. Some men believed the news media had it wrong. No white man would just hand over a country to black rule. It was something far beyond any imagining. It was impossible to understand for those who had grown up in Africa.

Then the same news kept repeating the information and we had to believe it. The blacks attacked the scattered whites in the vast land of rainforest and big rivers. Where the hell was their army? When would the blacks be driven off? Each day the news reports came in of whites being killed and women raped. Convoys of fleeing whites stopped by rag-tailed Congolese Army patrols and mass murder and rape done at the roadside. Those reports came to us in that echoing sports hall, while from nearby outside came the sound of rioting and shots of the police firing over the heads of the screaming black mob. Above all was the utter disbelief that anything like that could happen. This side of the border the agitating blacks were well under control; that would always be the case. The few police out there did not even need the might of the army to deal with the unrest.

They came through Kitwe, those sorry refugees, passing by in overloaded cars, many wearing bloody bandages and with grotesquely swollen faces all black and blue, all of them heading south away from the killing grounds. We stood and watched and wondered. The white men of the Northern Rhodesia Regiment had their suspicion of black rule firmly endorsed by the early Congo's massacres of the white Belgians. Outside the sports club grounds smoke from burning barricades rose and teargas wafted on the wind. But no one had been hurt or killed. The strangeness of it all was hard to grasp. Yet to a man the Territorials were sure that nothing like that could ever happen in Northern Rhodesia. Then a family in a Kombi was stopped near Chipinga in Southern Rhodesia and Petrus Oberholzer was murdered by what became known as the Crocodile Gang. The winds of change blew dark clouds over the sun.

It was not only the irritating call-ups that got to me. It was also the obsolete orders that had to be obeyed. Trained as a Bren gunner it was my lot to carry the machine gun on riot duty. The rules during civil rioting were very strict and British. We were permitted to shoot only when individually ordered by name to do so by the senior officer in charge. Before any force was used at all, the riot act had to be read three times over a loudspeaker and a large banner telling all to disperse unfolded. If ordered to fire then all expended cartridges were to be collected as evidence for the courts. We soldiers laughed, but it was rueful laughter as we knew we would be compelled to comply. The officers were bloody mad. How the hell do you collect cartridges from machine-gun fire? How do you identify spent brass as your own? The call to help the police never came so the order to fire was not given. So our discipline was not put to the test. The police made do with teargas launchers and long batons. My own discipline would have been sorely tested by any such orders.

It was the persistent call-ups, combined with stupidity of some of the orders and the strangeness of the new politics which was the deciding factor. The very high pay and bonuses on the copper mines meant there was plenty of money to spare. Many young miners of that wild time went off to Europe for a few years, travelled around, and had an extended holiday on the deep well of money. With two others from the mine as companions I booked on the *Windsor Castle* one way to England and left Africa to see some of the world. There were no plans other than to get away from the army. My experience of life was limited to how to hunt and fish and shoot guns. Maybe the best way for a young man to learn at the fleshpots of life is to begin with a clean slate. Begin with an open mind and with un-jaded taste. Excess quickly sates even the most robust appetite and enjoyment of excess lasts longer in the innocent.

The bitter resentment of military service was maybe misplaced. Throughout recorded history young men have been the mainstay of armies. There are valid reasons for this. Young men are physically capable of sustained labour. Young men do not understand death. Young men like playacting at being mature, grown men. In human males there is an instinctive hunting imperative that runs deep in the genetic makeup. Men all feel the innate urge to hunt and kill, and older men, the politicians, turn that urge to their advantage when they go to war with rivals. Everywhere the young are used when there is killing to be done. Young men are grateful for any small reward the elders deign to bestow on them; that reward is usually only false praise for being patriotic. When it is more than mere praise by the elders, when the reward is more material, young men line up in droves and offer to serve.

So it was that my twentieth year found me sitting on a deckchair aboard a liner heading for Europe. Big cities, wanton women, heavy traffic, nightclubs, and drugs were beyond my known, narrow horizon. Sitting on that deckchair was a big and strong farmboy, so inexperienced in life he thought nothing could scare him. The ignorant do not know what many things there are in life there are to fear. Work would surely not be a problem, as a learner official on the mine I knew all about ventilation, stope control and underground survey. What more could a man need to find work in England and Europe? The unknown has no terrors to those with no imagination. Life was good and sweet and the salty wind blew scent and suntan lotion across the rocking deck.

The anvil of life had so far only roughly shaped me and a final shape would take some time yet to emerge from the forge.

2

The steam train took five days to Cape Town and the liner twelve days to Southampton. That journey was the opening of Pandora's Box. I had never been anywhere with so many people gathered together in one place, nor had I ever dined in a room full of people with waiters serving. Suddenly I was in great demand by a dozen desirable girls who treated me like a prince and vied for my attention. One morning in her cabin an athletic, insatiable and very experienced woman showed me a side of sex that my wildest fantasies had not known. During those twelve days a lot of time was spent in a lot of different cabins eagerly learning what there is to know about sex. Cruise liners are that way for the young, giant floating sex shops. By the time the liner arrived in London the lessons were almost complete. For a while daily danger in the bowels of the earth and death vanished from my life and it was replaced by liquor, parties and sex, sex, sex. It was the rock and roll era, free love and flower power. It was all about travelling England and Europe in the relentless pursuit of sex. Pubic crabs and gonorrhoea were the ultimate punishment for excess in those days before AIDS, and were badges of honour.

The money ran out very soon after getting to London. The only work suitable for the uneducated colonial was on building sites, in pubs or as temporary labourers at catering functions. The rent for the bedsit room and gas for the weekly bath took a lot of the small wage, but the rest went on beer. Picking up cigarette stumps on the street so the remaining scraps of tobacco could be hand-rolled soon taught me that money was the key to high living. In Copenhagen, the city of no sexual hang-ups, working as a dishwasher in a hotel steakhouse showed me the more desirable a woman, is the more she exploits that desirability to squeeze the poor men who pursue her. It slowly dawned on me that there was a layer of society I could only dream of. Without money the door to that upper crust and the most desirable and beautiful women was locked. On the Copper Belt there was only a small population, and miners who had excess money were the upper class. Europe was no different and only wealth defined a person and his social status. This lust for money took me to the forests of Central Africa.

Humans eventually tire of excess and when they do boredom sets in. The final moment of *ennui* came one morning in Earl's Court in the Zambezi Club. I was sitting in the bar with one of those flat-tasting keg beers talking to an amply built English girl. An agreement was reached to spend the rest of the day in my bedsit. Sex was there for the taking. A sudden wave of boredom crashed over me as we got up to leave the club. I could not go on like this; endless drinking and fornicating with a string of complacent and undemanding, slightly eager girls. At the exit she turned left and I turned right, walked rapidly away without looking back and ignoring her calling. The airfare begged from my long estranged father bought a budget flight back to Salisbury. Two years on, having lived in London and Copenhagen and seen some of 'the world' my feet were again on Africa. The fresh air and nearly empty wide streets of Salisbury were unfamiliar and strange after the brown roar of the London traffic.

But the boredom continued; body and soul had steeped in excess for a long time. It took over two years to get bored with the civilized world and the fleshpots, bored with crowded cities and the roar of traffic. The DC-6 had taken three nights and two days to reach Salisbury. It stopped in Cairo, Nairobi, and Lusaka and then finally Salisbury. By then starvation had taken hold as I had no money to buy food and the budget flight did not serve any free; that was the only recollection of that flight home. Those days of excess in Europe were also part of the environment that formed the young me. But now back under the cool blue sky of the higveldt of Salisbury the only lasting legacy from the excess was an overwhelming desire to be rich. The role of a hard-working and dirt-poor farmer was not one that interested me. Money was an urgent desire; maybe the fleshpots of Europe still did guide my desires.

So it came about five years after graduating from school I found myself back living with my mother, a junior school teacher. My only formal qualification was a Cambridge School Certificate and with that there was no prospect of a cushy job and lots of money, even for a pampered white colonial. Each day the first thing done was a search of the newspapers for work vacancies. Some job interviews came and went without result. There were plenty of jobs available in the Civil Service which offered £30 a month gross, which equalled about a day's pay on the mines. The previous short stay with the tax people had convinced me I was no paper jockey. My mother was again agitating for university qualification. The need of a degree was not clear to me as I had already earned big money without it.

Northern Rhodesia was by now Zambia and Kaunda was president. Back in Mufulira, in the newly named country, the job previously held was offered back to me, but at a quarter of the previous money as "the mine has been Africanized." The winds of change blew the mining houses good fortune. Nothing else came up on the mines and the slow decay of black rule was already evident after only a short time in Zambia. It was easy to drive south and with no regrets. Zambia was never my home. Home was Southern Rhodesia and it was still white-ruled and would always remain so.

A friend called one day and invited me to join him at a nightclub. He was still on the Copper Belt and down in Salisbury on leave. We met and during the evening he introduced his date. She did not interest me and was not on my mind at all that night; I hardly noticed her, being busy with the seduction of my own woman. Some hours later a phone call came. The voice was familiar but I could not link the voice to a face so kept talking.

"Listen, when are you going to come and visit me?" She asked in that coy voice women reserve for these invitations.

"Listen, love, you know me, always forgetting the important things. I know I wrote it down but lost it. Tell me again where you stay." She told me, and then had to ask.

"When will I see you?"

"Today, this evening, make it 6pm. It's too long since we got together; make it 6pm, OK?"

That same night found me sweating and naked on an upholstered couch with an expert in the sexual art. The bodies of some women are just better fitted out for sex than others, and usually those women enjoy sex more, which also gives the man more pleasure. Until the door opened that evening I was not sure who she was. She turned out to be the woman my miner friend had brought to the nightclub date. She was married to yet another copper miner, Pete. Some days later after a long energetic session left me sweating heavily in the cool night air; I dressed and made for the door. The apartment block was in the avenues of Salisbury and jacaranda trees lining the streets perfumed the air. As I pulled open the door, her husband Pete arrived, stood with hand out, reaching to push the already opening door. As I stepped out he looked puzzled and stepped inside round my exit. I jumped the steps five at a time to my Triumph Tiger, and the exhaust of the motorcycle thundered as I gunned down the road into the sheltering night. It turned out to be a mistake to believe the aggrieved husband would not find me.

My life was in a limbo at the age of 23, partly moulded by circumstance and partly by environment. There was no direction or ambition beyond a yearning to be rich. Playing club rugby and water polo kept me strong and fit. Chance had seen to it that very little frightened me. My short adult life had brought more liaisons with women than most men manage in a long lifetime. Hunting game for meat was one of the things that kept life vaguely interesting. The travels had left a desire for other places. But here in the balmy small city despite the infrequent hunting trips, no money or travel meant boredom set in. How quickly that boredom was replaced with the dread of death! – knowing about real death means knowing about the death of man. Most species avoid killing their own. Man is not so inhibited. Hubris is a thing that infects all young men. The fact that in life learning never stops was not something I knew in those idle, bored summer days in Salisbury

Some things were clear to me, and living with mother was not an option except for a short time. No job and no money meant the ritual daily walk to the corner for a paper from the hawker. Then home to carefully read and reread the job vacancies. Several times I toyed with phoning up to enquire about farm assistant jobs, but then remembered the hard life, the isolation and loneliness of remote farms. A permanent air of gloom gripped me when an advert stood out in the vacancies page. It read something like this: "Fit young men wanted for exciting and dangerous work. High rewards for men with military training." No phone number was given but there was an address and an invitation to come to interview any morning during the next week. Time and circumstance, not willing choice, sent me off to a dirty, bloody little war. As the saying goes; life happens when you are busy with something else.

The office was in a small block on the road to the New Sarum airport on the outskirts of Hatfield, an almost rural suburb. Six or so other furtive-looking men were sitting waiting to be called for interviews, like dental patients. Quiet questioning confirmed that none of them knew any detail of the job on offer either. When called into the interview office they told me to sit on a hard wooden chair in front of a desk. There were three men the other side of the desk. None of them was familiar. The first impression that came into my mind was not good. The word 'bullshitters' flashed a warning in my mind. The main interviewer was Puren, who later turned out to be second-in-command to Hoare and in charge of the air force when it was eventually formed. The other two made so little impression I do not recall ever seeing them again after that day although they were probably present somewhere later. The windows were curtained over and the door carefully shut behind me. They first demanded everything that took place in the room be kept secret; no one was to be told anything. That was fine by me and certainly excited my curiosity

"Do you have any military training?"

"Yes, school cadets and call-up. Some territorial service and … "

"Fine, fine. Are you over twenty-one?"

"Over twenty-three …"

"Fine, fine. When would you be able to start?"

"Anytime but could you … I mean what …"

"Yes, yes. Remember this is top secret. What would you say to serving as a mercenary in the Congo?"

"How much … how much money … ?"

"£300 a month and £75 a day danger pay. Are you in?"

"Well, yes sure. Right on, sure."

"Report to the airport Friday at 1600. Bring only toiletries. Nothing else. You will not go through official customs or anything like that. Wear a suit; that is very important. Wear a suit and carry only a small bag. Did you get that? Do not, repeat not, tell anyone. What is your name? Right, send in the next man. 1600 on Friday, at the airport."

What the hell would anyone in similar circumstances say? In a daze I walked out into the sun and realized with a thrill of horror that I had no idea what the job would require, no idea at all. What the hell. Pay would be very high; what did £75 a day give over a month? That was all that mattered. It had been too long between big paydays. The pay offered was indeed high, but very little of it was ever seen. Right to the end of the contract most of the pay was stolen and eventually only a fraction of what was owed was paid over. That was in the unknown future. Saying yes after that offer of good money had taken only seconds. At last the sought-after prize was in grasp. In six months I would be rich again. The excitement of those easy riches burnt strongly in the bright Salisbury morning. The sky was a cloudless bright blue and the sun warm and yellow.

It was June 1964 when the road lay ahead, reaching into unknown lands. Bursting with excitement and needing to share it with friends I scratched money together. Friends were invited to join me at the nightclub for dinner and dancing, at my expense. In those far-off days money went a long way and £1 was enough for two to dine and dance at a nightclub. It was a good party and the only thing bothering me that night was which of the girls to choose for a final fling as a poor man.

The friends repeatedly asked what was going on, and the more I evaded the more they asked. The silly oath of secrecy held me back and all they learnt was a new job with heavy money had come up. By midnight the one girl, who was slim, strong and an acrobat in bed, was slow-dancing with me and we began to edge to the door. A newspaper hawker came to the club entrance with the early morning papers just then. The headlines of the *Rhodesia Herald* screamed "Mercenaries for the Congo recruited in city." So much for secrecy, and lots of screaming jokes followed from drunken friends. She was as insatiable as usual in bed that night, which is why she was chosen, and the sun came up before she went to sleep. It is a fact that during a war more male babies are born. A period of abstinence gives the sperm more of a male bias. If conception had taken place that night it would surely have been a female. A final night of sex is what all soldiers seek before going into action.

That hazy afternoon, having shortly before groaned out of bed and showered, I arrived at the Salisbury airport in a black suit, white shirt and tie wearing pointed leather shoes from swinging London and carrying a small plastic toilet bag with soap, towel, toothbrush and paste and a shaving kit; that bag was to be a most valuable possession in the months ahead. With head still buzzing with the previous night's excesses I wandered around and found some men similarly dressed, some I recognized from the recruiting office. The group milled about trying to find out what to do. There was no-one in charge and no-one gave directions. A glass door leading to the runway was opened in the terminal building and the group, by mutual consent, began to move out of the building. There were no government officials, no Customs.

It was still supposed to be secret, as the Rhodesian Government did not want it to be known mercenaries had been recruited in the country to help the Congolese Government. Rhodesia was then still in the British Commonwealth so the wishes would have been those of the British. The Rhodesian Government was not interested in intrigue. The British, like the Americans, preferred their opposition to the expansion of influence in Africa by China and Russia to remain clandestine. How does forming a regiment of white men to join a black army stay secret? The need to remain discreet was something the Americans carried though in the Congo for years. When they came back six months later the mercenaries endured a lot of media notoriety. Because of that, the return trip had to be through the transit lounge in Johannesburg and Customs in Salisbury, but it was merely a formality as both governments were happy to facilitate the returning men.

There had been a quick goodbye to my fearful mother and a shake of my brother's hand. In need of something to say, I whispered to him to tell my grieving mother if I did not come back that this was the way I wanted to go. That was just a grand gesture and not something sincerely meant, but that grand gesture coloured my brother's perception of me for all his life. The courage to tell him I made it up on the spur of the moment never came. Little things can have large repercussions.

The motley group wandered down the edge of a concrete runway towards a DC-3, a Dakota, and someone stuck a head out of the doorway of the aircraft and beckoned us to come up the steel steps into the aircraft. The flight from London to Salisbury had been my sole experience of aircraft. This old plane was rigged as military transport and a row of steel seats lined each side of the body facing inwards, and a wire for paratroopers' static lines ran down the middle of the roof. Standing at the cockpit door were a pilot and co-pilot in the blue uniforms of some private hire company who indicated we should sit and use the lap belts. Still no one in authority appeared and no orders were given. My seat let me look over my shoulder out a window at the wing of the aircraft.

The engines started and the plane vibrated. The wing and metal covering were shaking, and as the engines speeded up rivets in the wing vibrated loosely in the sockets and oil oozed out and streaked the wing. The engines roared louder and the plane trundled down the runway, still louder, as the wing flexed and bounced and suddenly the plane was off the ground floating in the air. My enduring hate of the DC-3 and flying in them began on that day. In later years as a member of the Rhodesian police, first in the paramilitary Support Unit and then fifteen years' service in the Police Anti-Terrorist Unit, a large part of my working life was spent bumping around tropical African skies in Dakotas. That first flight was followed by dozens of others over the next few months. My hatred was born of fear. They were not meant to fly, those squat, clumsy thick bits of metal. The Dakota has been in service from the 1940s to this day in many air fleets. My hatred was fuelled by the times the clumsy lumps of flying metal put my life as risk. Would knowing the future have turned me back from the steps of that aircraft? Not likely. Money is strong motivation for the young, immortal and poor.

Once off the ground air vents blew and circulated air inside the hot body of the plane and then the reek of alcohol became very strong. There were twenty or so men in the aircraft and most were drunk. I was sweating alcohol fumes in the humid air from the previous evening at the nightclub. Then the pungent reek of *dagga*, as marijuana is called in this part of Africa, clogged my nose. Smoking weed was illegal. Breaking the law still bothered me back then. Large brown-paper wrapped reefers were openly being passed around. Automatically my mind recoiled expecting someone in authority to step in. That bitingly pungent smell burnt into to my mind with memories of that day so that five decades later, the smell of dagga still recalls the Congo. Some women's perfumes are also evocative in that way. Bottles of brandy were also being passed around, with neat swigs taken from the neck.

Word went around that Johannesburg was the destination and that there transfer to another plane would take place. That city was several hours' flying time away in the Dakota. The pilots had shut the cockpit door and did not come out again. By the end of an hour many men in the plane were asleep, sedated by liquor and drugs. My shoulders pushed rigidly against the cold skin of the plane. Avoiding eye contact with increasingly pugnacious and drunk neighbours seemed to be a good idea. How would the next six months be? Doubts filled me but at no time was it an option to turn around and go home. Worried and scared by the bouncing flight, a stubborn streak of pride forbade me to give up. Then my feelings slowly changed from dread and doubt to excited curiosity. Whatever lay ahead, I was man enough for it; bring it on. Such are the fruits of ignorance.

The men on the plane held no fears for me although it was better to avoid confrontation. A quick inspection showed no one to be feared physically. They were a soft, unfit lot except for two or three ex-Rhodesian Light Infantry soldiers who were small, tough and wiry. The Saturday nights with Ron at the hotel on the Copper Belt had given me a discerning eye for good brawlers and there were none in this drunken bunch. Territorial service with the Rhodesian Army and the disciplinary methods of the British Army ingrained the need to obey. But one must respect a man before obeying him. No-one on the plane or before boarding gave any orders so there was no one to obey. Self-preservation was the imperative. As the plane wallowed through the African sky, the previous night and constant nervousness caught up and fitful sleep came.

During that flight something intangible present in the aircraft nagged my semi-conscious. There was a smell maybe, a vague almost physical thing hard to identify.

It was some time before I put a name to it. It was fear. It was terror. Fear of the unknown, fear of death mixed with the desire to live. That aura of fear put out by men near me was a constant companion for the next six months. It became a familiar if shadowy companion. Is there any time in life where man does not fear something? It seems to me that only when we are dead do we no longer fear anything. Fear motivates our lives and for the most part that fear is the fear of death and only in death is there relief. Ironically the closer death is the deeper the fear, and only in death no fear.

Sometime in the black night the plane bounced back to ground and lights streaked by the window. It turned and taxied for some distance with roaring engines. It stopped, someone opened the door and a ladder was put in place. The mob disembarked into the dark of the night and far away were the lights of a terminal. A voice came out of the dark. It was the voice of someone used to being obeyed and it ordered the mob to keep quiet. When they were, the voice went on. We were in South Africa but would not pass through Customs. We were to follow him quickly and board a plane to Kamina in Katanga. Anyone caught drinking or smoking dagga would be in trouble. Men around me muttered and some tried to stop lurching; clearly the owner of the voice would take no nonsense from anyone.

A larger aircraft loomed in the dark. It was a four-engined turbojet, an old DC-6 that saw much service in the ragged African airlines of the time. It had proper seats with clean cloth covers over them, magazines in the racks behind the seats and adjustable air vents. The mob shuffled along the aisle and sat down. Interior lights were off so it was dark inside. Seatbelt warning lights were the only light in the cabin. The voice again forbade the taking of drink or drugs, saying the aircraft would arrive at Kamina in Katanga early in the morning. The engines whined and the big plane shuddered, brakes released and it rolled forwards across a bumpy strip of tar. The plane twisted and turned and suddenly there were runway lights each side. The whine of the engines became a roar and it suddenly shot forwards and climbed rapidly. Misty white clouds swirled by the window, reflecting the lights of the big city below and then it was above the clouds and millions of stars were visible out of the window. Sometime into the flight sleep came again, a deep, exhausted sleep. Tomorrow would bring a new chapter of life.

3

The Katanga province of the Congo is in tropical Africa. It is a very desirable bit of earth, with rolling hills and forests of large trees; there is prime farming land and there are huge deposits of copper, diamonds, gold and many other minerals. In the early 1960s when the Belgians pulled out, leaving the white settlers to be slaughtered by the Congolese Army, Moise Tshombe declared Katanga a country independent from the rest of the Congo. A civil war was fought and eventually the United Nations sent troops to end the secession. Tshombe called in white mercenaries to wage war against the UN and Congolese Government for him. They were paid with revenue from the diamond fields, which also bought weapons and ammunition. After a few months Tshombe's dreams were ended by the UN and he went into exile.

In 1963 Patrick Lumumba, with the backing of the Russians, then engaged in cold war with the West and started a rebel movement in the Great Lakes area in northern Congo seeking to overthrow President Kasavubu. His warlord was one Pierre Mulele. Mobutu, who later ruled the Congo for many decades, was then an officer in the ragged army. Lumumba's movement made rapid gains against the weak government forces, who were more used to raping and looting than fighting. An arrangement was made between Tshombe and the government and he was installed as Prime Minister in the belief he would repel Lumumba. Tshombe once again turned to white mercenaries who had fought for him in the Katanga secession, to Mike Hoare, and Puren.

The DC-6 that landed in Kamina that autumn of 1964 carried on it the first major contingent of mercenary recruits for what was called 5 Commando Group of the *Armée Nationale Congolaise*. The language used by Belgian government officials was French. The new black rulers took on the language of the colonial master. Today French is the most widely spoken language in Central Africa. There were only one or two men with 5 Commando Group who spoke the language. Swahili could reach some of the population and a few mercenaries could speak that, but besides broken French many tribesmen spoke only a local tongue, of which there were many different ones. From the moment the plane landed there was a language barrier between the mercenaries and the local people. To understand another man, his thinking and actions, it is necessary to talk his own language.

Mike Hoare, the overall commander, and his second in command Puren, had arrived at the Kamina base some weeks before the main body of recruits. With them had come a dozen earlier recruited mercenaries, mostly from South Africa. A force

31

of some twelve men had been hastily put together and flown off to the north, to the Great Lakes, where an attack on the Lumumba rebels was carelessly mounted. Tshombe and the Americans needed the attack for political reasons; something to do with further funding. The attack was repulsed with some of the mercenaries wounded. It was badly planned and carried out by men reluctant to begin fighting as they had insufficient arms and no training. The wounded men wearing bandages, made from torn uniforms, arrived back at the Kamina barracks shortly after our first contingent arrived. They all looked exhausted and dirty in a wide assortment of tattered uniforms.

Curious to learn more about the enemy we, the new arrivals, talked to them. There was not much to learn. All they could say about the enemy was that they were black men with guns, followers of Mulele, who was fighting for Lumumba. The leader in the field of the rebel forces was Pierre Mulele. He, as so many before him in Africa had done, convinced his followers that taking potions supplied by his witchdoctors turned bullets into water. An enduring image comes to my mind even today of semi- naked men on the jungle tracks firing guns at the clouds and chanting "Mulele mia, Mulele mia". Mulele's water would protect them. It was as powerless against 7.62mm NATO ammunition as it was against the muzzle-loaders of the early settlers.

We learnt that day the rebels were generally called the Simba, which meant lion in the local language. They were totally untrained and had a motley collection of firearms. They looted, raped and murdered at will in all the towns they overran. They were mainly men from tribes who lived in the north of the country. Those wounded men at Kamina did not know who exactly they had attacked up at the Great Lakes; it had been at night with a sudden disorderly charge at a village from the cover of jungle which had been met with heavy return fire.

The scuttlebutt talk also claimed there were rebel youth wings, boys as young as ten or less known as the *jeunesse,* or youth in French. These juveniles were insanely murderous, far worse than the Simba. They did not have any moral restraint at all and killed and maimed for fun, and were often at the forefront when raping and murdering whites, but they were also at the forefront of murdering their own race once a town was taken. The youth were often used to spearhead an attack by the Simba rebels, a tactic that paid off against the Congolese Army as often the appearance of the vicious children would cause a mass retreat. Their mindless violence was feared all over the land. In normal circumstances shooting children would have given pause but they had such a reputation that they were to be shown no mercy. They were often drugged and mindless of danger.

There was a grain of truth in this, as there is in all such rumours. The youth wing did exist and had a bad reputation but that early information was highly embellished and not accurate. In later days the youth attacked a convoy of ours, but the attack was no different to any other Simba attack. They were no different than other Simba, only younger. They came down a jungle road running at our Commando that day, expecting us to turn and run away just like their misguided elders so often did. The outcome was the same: a heap of bullet-mutilated bodies on the road. In a land where there is no media or telephone, rumour is the currency.

Those wounded men at Kamina also told of their struggle to find arms, food and medical supplies. That remained a constant problem throughout the contract. The Americans helped, but medical provisions were always in short supply and consisted of nothing more than an American soldier's emergency pack or ration pack. The medical pack was just a wound dressing and morphine. They also supplied plenty of ammunition for 7.62mm and 9mm sub-machine guns and rifles but for any other calibre the mercenaries had to find themselves. Food was always in short supply. At first I believed these supply issues were nothing but teething problems and would pass. But problems of shortages are never solved in Africa. That truth was soon learnt. But all that was to sink home to us in the future.

That first morning, before meeting the ill-fated raid members, the mob was marched down the road to the derelict barracks still in the suits and ties they had arrived in, in the tropical heat and clutching the small bags we had been allowed to bring. The barracks which were to be home for a few days had once been a Belgian colonial army training base. They were built in a square around a courtyard, with three of the wings as living quarters and the other the kitchen and dining rooms. The first Congo mercenaries who fought during the Tshombe secession had made a stand at the barracks against the UN, and a long battle had raged. An Irish contingent was involved. Fighting stopped when it got dark and all involved got drunk together. Eventually the mercenaries were winkled out with light artillery. The place was a semi-ruin with the walls, windows and doors pockmarked with holes from rifle and artillery fire. Orders were given to find a room and rest and report to a drill square after lunch at midday. My chosen room, like all of them, was filled with rubble, but had a wire-sprung divan with a tattered bit of foam rubber over the wire. The toilet bag made a pillow, the suit jacket, tie and shirt went on the floor and I tried to catch up on sleep.

The tropical heat of midday woke me in a sweat and sent me in search of something to eat. From that first day to the last of the contract six months later that search for food was the daily routine. Get up and look for something to eat, day after day. After some rummaging around the buildings I found the kitchen where men were working at gas stoves of army issue origin. Food was a cup of coffee and several slices of stale bread and butter. Expecting nothing more, it was enough. I had braced myself for hardship when I got on the aircraft at Salisbury. In military service a soldier soon learns it is best to expect the worst. That way anything but the worst is really not too bad.

In shimmering heat and humidity men were idling around on the edge of the drill square in the centre of the barracks. No-one in authority was to be seen. This set the pattern for the entire contract; a loose hierarchy who seldom gave orders were nominally in charge. Neither the immediate commanders nor those a bit higher up ever seemed to know what the task at hand was. There was no clear objective other than to clear the country of the rebels of Lumumba and Mulele. It was left to the men on the ground to decide how that should be done. The unit commanders had no maps in an unknown country, seldom were in touch with headquarters and wanted only to get to the end of the contract with as little risk possible. Junior NCOs and the men under them thought likewise. That first morning all were waiting for Hoare and headquarters staff to give some clear orders. They never came.

As I sat on a low stone wall looking at the ground between my feet a pair of shiny calf-length boots stopped in front of me. I slowly looked up the camouflage clad legs and torso to see Pete, the husband cuckolded in the Salisbury avenues. He was neatly uniformed in camouflage and wearing a black beret cocked over one eye. A heavy revolver was holstered on his hip and there were sergeant strips on the shirtsleeve. In fighting mode at once, I felt regret that my career as a mercenary had come to such a short end; fighting with an NCO would surely be the finish. But his face split in a humorous grin and he stuck a hand out in welcome and we shook like old friends. The woman, he explained, was just one of three wives. He had not bothered to divorce or tell any of them about the others. He kept her on, he explained earnestly, because she was so good at sex. That left me with nothing to do but blush and agree.

After leaving Kamina I did not see Pete again until, a lifetime later, I saw him in the Ambassador Hotel in Salisbury. He introduced me to vodka and Coke, a drink that was an only favourite most of my life. He went mining in Matabeleland and to help pay his own mine expenses he worked part-time underground at the Wankie Coal Mine. The massive coal dust explosion in the 1970s that killed the entire working shift and closed a major section of Wankie was where he ended life. Hundreds died with him in that disaster; it takes a special type of madman to work on a coal mine.

Pete had come to Kamina some days earlier and was in charge of training. No uniforms had yet been received and no weapons or transport had arrived either. Pete had been given two weeks to complete training of the new arrivals. Another plane-load of men was expected the next day, so he would begin the physical training tomorrow. He invited me to drink beer with him. Food was scarce and there was no military equipment or communications, but beer was plentiful. Everywhere in the Congo that was always the way; bottled beer was always to be had.

We went to a lounge where a Scot had ensconced himself behind a small bar with a deep freeze full of beer which was selling for Congolese francs. All drank on tabs as no one had any of the local money, and the Scot trusted us to pay at some time. Later it became clear local money was not worth the paper it was printed on. I never found out what happened to that debt with the Scot or even his name. Later that evening we joined the inevitable Crown and Anchor school with our beers, playing with matches and again on a tab. So that first day as a mercenary ended with gambling and drinking late into the night, a late supper of tinned food, and a collapse on the noisy, uncomfortable bed in the steamy tropical night. Is this what they pay me for, was my thought.

In the morning, while the night mist was still curling up from the ground, a loud voice shouted, calling everyone to fall in for P.T. The men were still in the crumpled suits they had been wearing for some days already and my shoes were fancy leather pointed winkle-pickers. The one working outside tap supplied a long drink of water to rinse the foulness of cigarettes and beer away and then I fell in like a good territorial soldier. There were perhaps 50 men, all in civilian clothes. We were marched in a ragged mass a hundred metres to an assault course at the back of the old barracks.

Pete looked and sounded like a Regimental Sergeant Major in his uniform and with a big strong voice, all menace and command. Now that was better, almost like home. Sticks of five men were sent at a time to tackle the course. It had rope climbs and swings, wooden walls, deep ditches, barbed wire obstacles and every difficult object a vindictive army physical training instructor could think of. It was an ideal course for keeping highly trained and fit soldiers in shape. But the sweeping of the city streets, in civilian clothes, failed dismally to complete it. Being young, strong and fit I was determined to overcome, but the bile from the previous days and nights of excessive drinking soon rose and vomit spewed from the top of a wall climb.

Over the next few days that obstacle course became an object of extreme hatred. Everything that had made me reject the military call-ups years before was embodied in it; all the shouting, bullying, futile physical effort and the mindless obedience. As usual it was all for nothing. The Commando never had to do anything remotely involving physical exercise at any time during the contract. They were vehicle-borne most of the time and seldom even walked, never mind ran. That is the nature of all armies. Do as you are told, and never question. At the end of two days of training my clothes were stiff with dried sweat, salt and caked dirt, and my fancy leather shoes torn, scuffed and the heels worn off. There was mutiny in the air at being treated like a bunch of soldiers in detention barracks. That was the only point at which an option to return home was considered. Fortunately it did not last long.

It was then, in the nick of time for me, Hoare arrived back from somewhere with a handful of senior men. The angry men were formed up in ranks of three on the parade square for an address by Hoare. My first impression of him, the first word that came to mind was 'bullshitter' but that was followed at once by 'dangerous and strong'. Hoare had a natural commanding manner, one that induced obedience in any trained soldier. The speech was about what a fine body of men stood before him, the standard commanding officer pep talk. Then Commandos were formed and by virtue of my place in the parade, 51 Commando, the first to be formed, became my unit. New men had arrived almost daily and two other Commandos were formed at the same time, 52 and 53. Each unit had about 30 men. More platoon-sized units were formed over later weeks and months, but those new units had no contact with 51 Commando. Now the drill, marching and assault course were done as a Commando, nominally under the orders of NCOs of 51 Commando.

At no time during the six months did Hoare issue orders directly, or to my best knowledge indirectly, to the Commando. Most of the time he was invisible, and when he did appear at the same place as us, he had no orders. Several times he addressed assembled men but at those times he made speeches and did not issue orders. He had a group of men who went everywhere with him, as a sort of headquarters staff. Most of them remained unknown to me. I knew neither what they did nor what rank they carried. There is a theory that no more than twelve men should be involved in military or organized actions. More than twelve members makes a unit hard to control. Which is why there were twelve disciples and are smaller basic units in all armies. Certainly the Commando split into small units. The units that did most of the fighting were generally formed of eight or so men to two Jeeps

The lunacy that marks military life varies little from one army to the next. One morning orders were given to form into columns of three, that were then marched quickstep down the road to a small village over fifteen kilometres away. It was very hot and humid, men were still in battered civilian clothes and there was no rest and no water. Uniformed men with sergeant's insignia shouted and badgered everyone to keep going. The route march undertaken was to present the Commando to senior officers of the Congolese Army. The man in front of me on that long, hot march was a Greek who lived on drugs, and was in a highly excited state the whole march. During the forced six-hour march he constantly sang and shouted incoherently, and when his energy waned he swallowed more pills. He vanished after that day but on that idiotic march he gave me something to concentrate on beside the pain of my feet.

The column arrived at buildings near the road edge in a small village and some uniformed black men came out. They wore the insignia of high rank on shoulders and caps, lots of yellow braid and red crowns. Each of them wore dark glasses and the uniforms were dirty, creased and ill fitting so all the insignia of rank looked shiny, clean and very new. The Congolese officers stood looking at the column for a short moment and then slouched back into the building they had come out of. The Commando about-turned on orders and marched rapidly for three more hours back to the barracks.

My own endurance with all things military was being stretched to the limit. The Commando was still being treated worse than if they were detention barracks inmates; starved, abused physically and still no arms or uniforms had been issued. This was not an army recruitment camp, most of us had already been trained and it was not what we were willing to accept. Many men began to make plans to get on the next plane out. Some had already done so. Then, about ten days after arriving, arms and ammunition were issued, which began a change in attitude. Progress renewed energy. FN 7.62mm assault rifles were issued, the same rifles the Rhodesian Territorial's had recently converted to. The bolt-action Lee Enfield .303, or similar rifles, had been standard issue to the British forces for maybe a hundred years, but today automatic fire and large-capacity magazines have taken over in most armies. A gun in his hand changes a man.

Four spare magazines came my way during the issue of rifles; they were simply taken from the crate while the men issuing weapons were not looking; previous military training has advantages. In the coming days spare magazines became the local gold, and the more you had the richer you were. This was a manifestation of the constant fear; plenty of magazines meant lots of ammunition, which meant you were able to defend yourself longer. A fallacy but one most believed in. The sound of your own rifle firing is very assuring. Some men taped magazines back to back to enable a faster reload. That method usually causes jams as the one magazine throat is at all times open to dust and mud. Any magazines left unguarded, or out of sight, were likely to be stolen. As all the magazines were identical it was impossible to know your own unless marked in some way, but even when that was done the thefts went on. It became second nature to keep your own loaded magazines nearby at all times even when sleeping.

It took days of diligent scrounging to find a pair of camouflage trousers and a camouflage paratrooper's jacket, the one with the tail that fastens between the legs when jumping out of an aircraft to stop it from flapping in the wind. The jacket worn open without a shirt was ideal for the fetid climate. For the duration of the contract no uniforms were officially issued and the only way to get clothing was to loot and steal. This included boots. One day at the airstrip I got lucky and bought a pair from a US Marine who was guarding ammunition resupply aircraft. For them he accepted the couple of Rhodesian pounds still left in my pocket.

The same clothing had to be worn for weeks at a time without washing as most of us had only one set, and we soon got used to the smell of each other. Hygiene was far from a major concern. Men washed clothing and bathed when they could, but most of the time chances to do so were few and far between. Getting new clothing was also very seldom and far between. When a rare chance came the uniform was washed while the wearer was naked and then quickly dried in the sun and put on again. There was no standard uniform but most men managed to find army camouflage or khaki items. Some wore steel helmets, most had boots. After a while it became easy to recognize someone from the distance by the individual uniform he wore, it was changed so seldom.

The commanding officer of 51 Commando, who held the rank of lieutenant, was a tall thin Englishman with a dark-skinned, delicate face and who had been in an elite British Guards regiment. His name was Wilson. He had no experience of handling the riff raff he now had to command, and was short of ideas on how to do it. He expected all men to be gentlemen. What was he doing here, so far from his own land and environment? But as I never spoke with him that remained a mystery; he was clearly out of his depth but, like all professional British soldiers, fearless and led from the front. Those attributes alone made the men he nominally commanded respect him.

There were two sergeants with 51 Commando and the one who controlled the section I found myself in was called Ginger. He had a flaming red beard and a bushy head of red hair. His skin was pale and freckled; he was a big, muscular man, who spoke softly and then never said much. Like all the other NCOs he gave few orders. Those in command knew as little as the rest of us about what the goings-on in the country were or where we were going next. Not always, but most of the time, their commands were no more than requests. That was because they feared the men they commanded. Everything ran on that one constant: fear. The few NCOs formed a small, tight knit unit of their own for mutual protection, as did the rest of the men of the Commando.

It happened suddenly and unexpectedly, two weeks or so after landing in Kamina, and the fear of the unknown intensified. Orders were shouted by the headquarters staff early one morning for 51 Commando to assemble on the parade square. There, Wilson said, in his soft modulated voice, the Commando was going to fly north and go into action against the rebels. He did not know, he said carefully, where the landing would be as that was to be decided while in the air, and according to the ground situation. It would only be possible to say where exactly the airfield was on arrival. The same would apply as to where exactly the rebels were. Countrywide communications were bad. The town we were heading for had apparently been secured by the Congolese Army. It was near the Congo River but that was also not certain. The Congolese garrison would be responsible for the issue of vehicles and other stores on arrival. Later that morning 51 Commando boarded a lumbering Dakota flown by men with American accents who claimed to be anti-Castro Cubans, and flew north into the unknown. That Dakota took the Commando to an unknown destination to fight an enemy, as yet unseen, and they had to rely on the Congolese Army for vital supplies. Not very encouraging, yet we were all glad to see the back of the tattered Kaminaville barracks.

4

The land below the aircraft became greener as we flew north and eventually the Dakota was droning over a dense, dark green sea of jungle through which only silver strings marking rivers showed. The land of Katanga had been open savannah with rolling hills and open woodlands, similar to the Zambian Copper Belt. Now there were no roads or built-up areas to be seen, just dark green jungle from horizon to horizon. The Commando was heading toward the equator so inside the aircraft's metal shell the heat of the overhead sun could be felt. A rich, damp rotting vegetation smell came up from the jungle and filled the plane. It flew low above the jungle and at intervals parrots and other birds could be seen to fly above the green canopy in a brief flash of colour before diving back out of sight.

I intermittently looked down at the forest while cleaning my rifle, and oiling and cleaning the ammunition in the spare magazines. That activity helped distract from the wallowing up and down of the aircraft in the hot turbulent air. Each time an air pocket dropped the aircraft my backside lifted off the seat and I had to swallow hard. In the next few months I grew to detest that clumsy-looking, noisy Dakota and the pseudo-Cuban pilots who flew them so carelessly. There was no way of avoiding travel by air as the road network, never extensive, was now reverting to jungle. Maintenance had not been done for years and the majority of dirt roads were rain-soaked soft muddy ditches. Air transport and the riverboatss were all that was feasible

That particular Dakota had been converted to a civilian passenger plane with two rows of seats each side of a central aisle and sitting in the seat alongside me was Boeta. Boeta became a staunch friend and companion. It was difficult to say why; he was a violent and dangerous man but better to have as a close friend than as an enemy. One morning in the barracks at Kamina the sound of gunfire came from behind a building and on investigation I discovered Boeta. Firing a pistol at a steel helmet on the ground was a burly, round-shouldered man in green army clothing. When he saw me he stopped shooting and gave a thin smile and looked me over thoughtfully. His eyes were wolf grey and the beret on his head was turned inside-out and looked like a brown mushroom. The shooting was a test, he explained, to see how bullet-proof the steel helmet was. Bloody useless was his opinion. Around him was a tangible aura of supreme confidence. When the other recruits were angry and annoyed at the circumstances, he was cheerful and eager.

"Where you from," he asked, as his grey eyes measured me.

"Farmboy, been all over really. You know, Europe, Copper Belt, hunting."

"Where did you hunt?" The eyes left me and went back to the steel helmet and he shot at it a few more times as he listened to me.

"Been there done that. I'm Boeta," he stuck out his hand. "Ever shot a kaffir? No? Only game, hey?" His thin smile flashed briefly. "Those are one fucked-up pair of shoes. Come, let's find you a pair of boots. Come with me."

In his room he rummaged in a broken cupboard and took out a pair of black military boots. They were a bit too small but I made do until the Marine had sold me another pair soon thereafter.

Boeta was a nerveless and totally ruthless man, who was in his element with a gun in hand. Many years later, while in the Rhodesian police, his criminal record was of interest to me. It was a long one and mostly for crimes of violence. By then he had been a companion for some years and the criminal record fitted with my knowledge of him. He was a man out of his time; he should have lived in the days of freebooter pirates or Western gunslingers. His ideal time would have been when men settled arguments outside in the street with violence, the old way. In an argument he was the one who kicked over the table and produced a gun to shoot down any opposition. Killing another man was, to him, merely a way of solving a disagreement. Anyone who thwarted him was in danger of being the target of his instant rage.

He was quick to anger, and once he was aroused did not tolerate any opposition whatsoever. When angry his face screwed up like a baby about to cry. The wolf eyes narrowed and he frowned hard. The full soft lips pouted and his shoulders hunched even more. When in such an aroused state he killed at the blink of an eye. His criminal record showed the law had failed to restrain his passions. Now in the Congo there was no law. The law was that of man versus man, winner takes all. Many times in the next few months there was reason to be glad he counted me a friend. In the days ahead we insured each other against fellow drunken, doped men who also murdered on a whim.

Boeta eventually signed up for four contracts in a row and on the second one, some months after I had returned to a normal life, he visited a nightclub in Leopoldville. The jazz band refused to play the music he requested. It was in the early hours of the morning so he would have been very drunk. He opened fire on the offending band with an FN on automatic fire and killed them all, as well as a couple of other patrons. The one band member turned out to be a relative of a high-ranking government official so Boeta was arrested, tried and sentenced to death. A week later he was back with his Commando; the funds he had accumulated from looting had allowed him buy his way out of it all.

On that Dakota on the way to war most of that was still in the future but instinct said to remain his friend. He hunched his shoulders, pressed his face to the window and looked down at the jungle. He turned to me in the next seat and grinned, noticing my anxiety as the plane dipped and banged in the air pockets.

"Don't like flying, Smiler?" He whistled tunelessly through his teeth, and then went on. "A fucker on the ground with a FN could shoot this thing out the sky. Standing down there in the trees he could take the whole fucking thing out of the sky, bang, bang. Any hunter could. Pilot and co-pilot and boom the thing crashes in the tees. Too fucking low for sure. What's the matter Smiler?"He grinned and whistled some more. "Tell you what, both those arsehole pilots are pissed, that's for sure. If they were sober they would not be flying so low. Wonder if the rebels have heavy machine guns. Boom, boom, boom. Don't worry Smiler, don't worry." He laughed shortly. My nickname Smiler came from my sometimes fixed smile when frightened, and once he used the nickname it stuck.

After an unknown time that seemed days the Dakota landed on a short, bumpy wet and muddy airstrip in the rainforests somewhere in central Congo. At that stage the Commando still had no idea of where exactly this airstrip was. Wilson and the sergeants said nothing on landing. The men climbed out of the plane and as soon as all were on the ground it took off and vanished south in the humid air. A battered green army troop carrier with a pair of buck horns mounted on the front of the radiator came out of the jungle onto the airstrip and stopped where the Commando were gathered. Some ragged Congolese Army soldiers shambled over and talked to Wilson. They spoke French, as did all the local government officials. Wilson and one or two others in the Commando spoke a little French. Then the Commando crowded on board the truck which drove only a short distance before a small village appeared in a clearing in the jungle. The village was made up of pretty, pastel-painted brick houses with neat fencing and gardens. There were no people to be seen. The truck went down one of three streets and came to a small hotel, with the name of the hotel on a board above the main door, a French name.

The hotel was not big and the thirty-odd men of the Commando filled it. A worried looking middle-aged Belgian couple came fearfully to the truck to greet the disembarking men. There was some discussion; the couple wanted to know how payment was to be made. Surely they were not expected to supply free board? Wilson talked with the Congolese and an official-looking document was produced and filled in with a pencil stub and signed by a Congolese with gold braid on his shoulders. It was an official requisition. No-one present believed it would ever be honoured and the owners looked resigned and waved the Commando in. The allocated room had air conditioning and a bathroom. Looking back later it came to me what a miracle this small inn was. Its isolation saved it from the mayhem that had swept the rest of the Congo. For some reason the Congolese Army had not looted it. As a requisition had been given, and accepted, perhaps the local commander still believed in some sort of law and order. The electricity plant still worked and the owners, eternal optimists, went on as normal, expecting guests to return one day. Big wooden signs in the gardens marked where the equator ran through the grounds. Lush, tall jungle crowded to the edges of the clearing of the small village. I felt the jungle was waiting for the humans to leave and then it would soon erase their puny efforts.

In the late afternoon the Commando went into the jungle, following a path to a small river where black water ran swiftly between overgrown banks. Homemade targets were stuck up on trees and for the first time weapons were fired in practice. Relief flooded through me when my rifle was found to be in good condition. The stock and butt showed signs of hard use which had been a reason to worry. It shot straight to point of aim and gave no hint of jamming. Automatic rifles were still foreign and new to me and at that time I felt a bolt action would have been a better choice. That was my feeling then but it soon changed. It was not long until the automatic became so familiar that any other sort of rifle was alien.

As other soldiers found, it did not take long to adapt and grow to like the 7.62 FN. It was a rifle which had been purpose-built from scratch as a military weapon and designed to take abuse and still function. Carefully cleaning the rifle again, I watched the Commando practise. It became obvious that the insistence of military training by the recruiters had been fiction. Some were clearly new to firing a rifle, any sort of rifle. Some were, as usual, drunk or high on dagga. Untrained men tended to flinch and jerk while firing, causing shots to scatter far and wide. Some men spent the entire six months drunk or drugged. Some of them lasted only days and were then sent out of the country, while others lasted the entire contract.

That day the men of 51 Commando were mostly strangers to me and only a few names matched faces. It took weeks before the men became recognizable and had names. Knowing someone by name sets an onus. Those who went home early never had names I knew, only those who lasted some time. All the men soon formed into small, mutually protective groups and those outside your group were merely men in the same boat, almost strangers. All were there for the money and at the outset they took steps to stay alive to enjoy a payday. The group was a Commando in name only, and it turned out that it was each cell for themselves, at all times. Boeta and I had already, at Kamina, formed a small cell which endured, slightly expanded, to the end of the contract. The cell grew and shrank but never more than two other men joined us.

The rest of that day was spent loafing at the small hotel. It was very hot and humid almost beyond endurance, and sweat kept bedraggled, makeshift uniforms wet through and dark. The new boots were a very big change from the battered winkle pickers; I felt sorry for some of the Commando who still wore civilian shoes. My boots were waterproof and comfortably worn in, especially welcome now when it rained a lot of the time. All day there was traffic between the hotel and the army barracks nearby in the steaming jungle. Wilson and the sergeants came and went several times. From odd bits of conversation I overheard it was possible to glean that our commander was trying to obtain uniform, transport and ammunition. It seemed the Congolese Army were reluctant to part with anything. How they expected the Commando to go into action without the necessary stores was a mystery. When things on the ground became clearer after some weeks, the situation was easy to understand. We had to adapt to the African way.

Until that day the Mulele rebels, the Simbas, had swept away all before them. The ragged, ill-disciplined Congolese Army had offered no opposition to them anywhere. For some miraculous reason the telephone system still worked intermittently in most parts of the country. The Simba rebels took advantage of this to call up a garrison in the way of an advanced warning to tell the commander an attack was to be launched. That phone call was enough to ensure the Congolese Army melted away in the night, heading south in a panicked rush, leaving the barracks empty and the local population unprotected. When the rebels arrived in the abandoned town an orgy of rape and looting took place and any straggling soldier falling into their hands was put to death. The lucky captives were shot but most were tortured to death. That was the reason why local garrison refused to supply stores. There was plenty of spare transport and weapons at the barracks but the Congolese Army were deathly afraid to give stores away and find shortages when the expected and imminent rebel assault did come. The rebels were driving south rapidly, so rapidly that their exact location was not known. No phone call had yet been made but the local commanding officer obviously expected one soon.

At midday the next morning orders were given to us by Wilson, speaking quietly and clearly, to march on the army garrison. Wilson ordered the Commando to take over some of the Second World War American Willys Jeeps and two big trucks. The trucks were apparently already loaded with stores including boxes of ammunition and rifles, intended for the retreat. The weapons were FN assault rifles and French MAT 49 9mm sub-machine guns. There were also cardboard boxes of spare uniforms and ammunition. Once the transport had been commandeered, Wilson ordered that it was to quickly be driven back to the hotel where the Commando's odds and ends were to be loaded for immediate departure north. That quiet modulated voice sent shivers of fear and excitement through me. Any Congolese Army member who objected was to be dealt with by using what force was necessary. There was no other choice, Wilson carefully explained, as the Army was obstinate and repeatedly refused to equip us even when his orders had been confirmed. Any questions? There were hundreds in each man's mind, but none was raised.

The few black privates put up a token objection as the Commando took over the vehicles standing at the barracks. None of their officers were to be seen. The transport was lined up in rows, fuelled and pointing towards the road leading south. The black soldiers were easily waved away with a rifle used to indicate 'stand aside'. There was a lack of any resistance. Our newly acquired convoy then drove to a filling station in the village where there was still some fuel in the pumps. The fuel tanks of four Jeeps and two three-ton trucks, Swedish-made Scania, were filled to the brim. Empty petrol drums, all that could be found, were also filled and put on trucks. Wooden ramps were used to roll the heavy drums on to the trucks. No-one came out to claim payment for the fuel and no arrangement for payment was attempted. Our first looting job had been easy and quick.

Leaving the pretty little village on the equator the new convoy took the road north, the road which eventually led to war. On the road to that war my inventory was a 7.62mm FN assault rifle and four spare twenty-round magazines, a pair of boots and worn-out socks, green army trousers and a green paratrooper jacket. Personal kit, my only other possession, was a small plastic toilet bag. The order of march was Wilson and the two sergeants in the lead Jeep, and the rest of the Commando distributed at random on the following vehicles. Of the thirty-odd men maybe ten were very drunk or drugged with dagga.

A supply of dagga had been located at the outskirts of the village, so a big black iron trunk full of the narcotic weed was on one of the trucks. A wisp of fragrant white smoke trailed the convoy as it drove through the tunnel the road made through the tropical jungle on the constantly wet road. On the way to war the enemy were still a totally unknown entity, what they looked like, what arms they had or exactly where they were. My position in the Jeep was behind Boeta, who was driving, hunched eagerly forward over the steering wheel. Boeta's web belt was crammed with ammunition pouches and an automatic pistol in a holster. The inside-out beret, his signature, was jammed tight on his head. A tuneless whistle came through his teeth. The terror that gripped the rest of the men only caused him excitement. His fearless enthusiasm gave me some confidence and put a different slant on what I thought and expected.

The arms and ammunition question plagued every mercenary throughout the contract. They often had to make do with what was collected from the dead, from searching army barracks deserted by the Congolese Army or from the occasional clandestine donation by the Americans. The Americans, represented by the CIA, flew in to all the landing strips retaken from the rebels as soon as they were secure. When it could be done without making it obvious supplies were given to the mercenaries, but normally these supplies were ammunition. The Americans backed the Congolese Government of Tshombe but did not want to be seen to supply arms, so they did it in a manner they thought clandestine. The Americans were afraid to provoke the Russians and get them involved on the side of the Simba rebels.

This was strange as the rebels were openly and obviously supplied and backed by Russia. Today a Lumumba University stands in Moscow. How did the Americans think that backing a war in Africa could be kept secret from Russia? When a town previously held by rebels was retaken the first aircraft to land on any nearby airstrip was American. Those inevitable near-to-town dirt strips were used by American planes which landed CIA agents to gather first-hand information. That information could have been fed to them on two-way radio by the mercenary forces far more easily. Some of those flights off-loaded arms and ammunition always with instruction to the mercenaries to keep quiet about what was being done. When a plane landed and dropped its cargo there was always a curious crowd of locals watching from the edge of the nearby jungle. What sort of mentality did the CIA have to think the crowd watching the planes land and take off saw nothing and said nothing?

At some of the towns retaken from the Simba stocks of weapons were left behind in erstwhile barracks by the fleeing Congolese Army. The abandoned weapons ranged from pre-First World War vintage to modern Belgium and French-manufactured arms. For the most part the Commando carried the 7.62mm Belgian-manufactured FN rifle or a 9mm MAT 49 French-made sub-machine gun, with older weapons ignored. There were plenty of the Russian AK-47 assault rifles to be had but they fired a smaller cartridge than the NATO 7.62mm and using the heavier ammunition gave a man more confidence in a firefight. This is one time size did matter and the larger round could shoot right through the pole and mud huts of the villages that lined the jungle tracks. An assortment of sidearms of all calibres from across the world were carried; each man selected a personal favourite as his handgun. A Colt revolver, .357 Magnum, was my handgun of choice as it was powerful and jam-free, which automatics are not. The Congolese Army issued no side-arms to its soldiers. Making do with what could be found is the way all African armies work. Being members of a dysfunctional African army was hard at first but 51 Commando soon adapted as there was no other way, and arms and ammunition were life.

5

Leaving that isolated and pretty little village on the equator, the Commando headed north towards the Congo River. The village we left was soon forgotten and the name slid into obscurity. There were many such places, small communities in a jungle clearing visited for an hour or two, places whose names we never discovered. The inhabitants had gone away or were in hiding. The Simba advance had been generally south from the Great Lakes region and down the Congo River, which runs in an east to west loop biased to the north. The ultimate aim of the Simba was to advance downstream to Stanleyville, the second largest city in the county and then carry on downriver taking the capital Leopoldville. The river was navigable between the two towns, which were many hundreds of kilometres apart. The only viable route between the two big cities was by riverboat. The roads were gone and the railway had long been suspended. The Congo is twice as large in area as South Africa and the two major towns roughly at opposite ends of it.

I remember the sound of myriads of birds singing waking me that last morning on the equator as I lay in my soft bed under a mosquito net. A look out the window revealed scores of yellow weaver birds in a clump of bamboo in the hotel grounds, a colony busy working on yellow grass nests that festooned the bamboo in such numbers some fronds bent low under the weight. That memory of the weaver birds became a distant one very soon. But today I think back and wonder if it would be possible to visit that hotel again, speculating if it still exists. Most likely it has been reclaimed by the jungle and the people who once lived there have faded from memory.

The Commando was on the road going northwards in the hope of meeting the advancing Simba. That road ran through the equatorial forest which was wet and dripping from the rain falling at intervals all day in warm showers. The rank and file had no access to the map Wilson now carried and so did not know the destination he had in mind. No direct orders had been given. The men got in their vehicles and followed the lead Jeep, which carried Wilson and the two sergeants. Before leaving my FN and spare magazines had been nervously oiled again; a good thing in all the damp. The rifle was cocked with the safety on. My position was behind the driver of a Jeep third from the front of the convoy. The back seats had all been removed and the steel wheel arch did duty as a seat. The roads had not been repaired in years and the Jeeps were war issue with heavy-duty springs. The discomfort at least distracted partially from the building fear. We could see only a short distance into the green wall of the rainforest on each side of the road. Thick undergrowth grew in profusion where the trees had been cut to make way for that road, where extra sunlight now fell. A few well-trained men could have wiped out the entire convoy in minutes by firing small arms from a well-laid ambush.

Later in the morning the advance reached another small village set out in European fashion in a clearing in the forest. The village was also a handful of brick houses set each side of two intersecting roads. At the entrance to the town, two hundred metres out, there was a makeshift block across the road manned by ragged and visibly scared Congolese Army troops. The roadblock was a telephone pole laid across two petrol drums blocking the road. This was and still is the standard roadblock throughout Africa and they proliferate in all the countries where law and order is a distant memory. As the convoy entered the small town two Catholic priests appeared at the side of the road in long white robes in the yard of one house and Wilson went off to talk with them.

From the waiting vehicles we saw Wilson and the sergeants served with tea and rusks. Having had not eaten all morning the men decided to look for food, got off the Jeeps and picked bananas from another nearby yard. Soon all the Commando joined in the scramble for food. There were bananas and pineapples, which were to be the most reliable food source in the weeks ahead. Our commander was sitting at the table on the veranda of a house talking animatedly and the priests looked glad to see him. A while later Wilson came to the banana-skin-littered road and told us we would sleep there for the night and the next day's advance would be to the nearby riverside town of Lisala. Many years later I discovered that Lisala was the birth place of Mobutu, who, after the mercenaries had captured and left the town, arrived to extract vengeance on all. Wilson told us the missionaries said Lisala was in rebel hands. The priests were also gravely concerned for colleagues at the Catholic mission in the town.

That night a first acquaintance was made with outsized mosquitoes which patrolled the rainforest in uncountable numbers. Sleeping on the floors of two empty houses most men had no blanket or ground sheet; sleeping on the ground when hunting was the norm, so to me it was no hardship. The hardship came from the insects. They arrived in thousands, the whine in the night sounded like a jet engine warming up. Striking out with a hand in the dark of the room meant connecting with a score of insects at each sweep. Without some sort of cover, sleep became impossible and eventually I found a dirty scrap of blanket in one of the rooms. I lay down again with my boots on, and covered my head and shoulders with the material. The mosquitoes bit through my shirt and trousers but at least in lesser numbers than when feeding on exposed flesh. It was hot and humid and noisy with the loud cursing from other men.

Chippy and Snooky the two ex-Rhodesian Light Infantry soldiers, small wiry men who loved military life, they were in their element. Hard times made them fall back on learnt lessons. They rolled and lit two massive cigars of dagga and soon the room was filled by a haze of the sweet-smelling smoke. That helped chase the insects away, that and the slightly cooler midnight air. In the early hours of the morning eventually sleep came. All were covered in a red rash of bites come the morning sun.

At first light we were up, bleary-eyed and hungry. There was still no food, and only water was found to drink. The bananas had all been reaped the previous night. Chippy, Snooky and others used dagga to stave off the hunger. Wilson again mounted the front Jeep with his senior men and signalled with a wide wave of his arm for the rest of us to follow. I got on the Jeep gripping my rifle hard and the small convoy went on north towards the town of Lisala. The wet, muddy road still ran through a dark green tunnel with heavy undergrowth either side and the branches of the taller trees almost meeting overhead. The air was warm with a morning mist drifting up off the road. No one felt like talking. There was no way of seeing what was about to happen. We did not know the enemy, didn't even know what they looked like. To us they were 'the Simba rebels'. Every man was tense and like me had rifles firmly gripped in sweating hands. Trying to see ahead through the undergrowth was unsuccessful as the jungle was a solid mass. My head was turned uncomfortably sideways at right angles on my neck as the steel seat faced the side of the road and I was looking forward. It was only possible to see only the few metres of road directly ahead of the Jeep.

The sun had risen to nearly overhead, a silver ball in the steamy sky, when the lead Jeep stopped and Wilson got down and signalled to the Commando to get off the vehicles and walk. The men formed a loose column across the red mud of the narrow road. The road was one vehicle wide so the men could only advance comfortably four or so abreast. The column stretched back fifteen metres from the front men to the back men. A moment of panic totally flooded my senses and made me blind for a moment. It was pure fear, fear of the unknown, and my mind screamed that the black rebels would capture, torture and kill us slowly. Each side of me soldiers were wide-eyed with the same fear. That moment of sudden panic before combat was normal, I later learnt. Boeta at my right shoulder was grinning in anticipation, eagerly watching the road ahead, hunched forward over his rifle in anticipation. He was whistling that part hiss of his through his front teeth and when he grinned widely at me my panic partly vanished. That was the first but not the last time the fear of combat and death gripped me, that blind panic of not knowing what to expect and feeling what was coming might overwhelm. Later it became as usual as a sneeze, something anticipated and normal.

A bullet hissed overhead and then a rifle cracked far away in the forest. Both were sounds which also later became daily routine. Next a deep bass chanting broke out ahead on the road through the stillness of the still curling road mist. There was shrill shouting, with more rifle shots and bullets hissing and cracking overhead. At the van of the advance on foot Wilson and the lead men were cresting a small rise and they now stopped, looking at something the other side of the rise. Some of the men behind them crowded forward and joined the bunch at the crest. About a dozen men of the Commando stood on or near the crest with the rest bunching up unsighted behind.

The rifle fire and shouting from beyond the crest intensified. It was hard to tell if bullets were near or far; at that stage I had not yet learnt to distinguish the sound of near misses from far ones and the whiplash of all shots sounded terrifyingly near. Wilson shouted an order which was hard to hear above the rudely loud rattle of gunfire. The men with him in the van on the crest raised weapons and the jungle began to vibrate and the air shudder to the thunder of a dozen heavy 7.62mm assault rifles firing rapidly. Some men further back on the road turned and fired into the jungle in blind panic. The crack of the bullets overhead and through the foliage was easily mistaken as fire coming in from the jungle near the road. Boeta ran forward as the firing began, knelt at the crest to fire carefully aimed shots. There was nothing in my sight to shoot at and my army training held me from firing at nothing. There was no room at the firing point ahead where men were already standing shoulder to shoulder on the road. The best thing to do seemed to be to face the green wall and look for a target. The maniacal thunder of firing lasted only short minutes, but time was distorted and it seemed a lifetime. Then silence, absolute and eerie silence. No silence is deeper than that which follows a lethal firefight.

The leading men began to go over the crest still in a solid mass stretched across the road shoulder to shoulder. Above the ringing in my ears came the distant sound of heavy trucks growling through the trees, the funnel of the jungle-enclosed road magnifying the intensity of sound. Passing over the crest the slight valley on the other side of the high point came into view. There, about fifty metres away, lay an untidy pile of bodies, a heap of sprawled corpses. The rebels had been gathered in a group around a witchdoctor and our bullets had cut them all down within touching distance of each other. As my eyes took in the scene and my mind made sense of it, two heavy trucks slowly came in sight on the forested road further away down the funnel of the track, packed with men. The men were cheering and chanting loudly and making ululating sounds. It sounded like a crowd at a football match whose side had just scored a goal. Men were leaning out from each side of the trucks, waving weapons and hands in triumphant manner. Some sat on the roof of the trucks from where they waved with both hands.

What the hell is this? That was the only question possible in all our minds. The driver of the leading truck advanced to a point where he saw the bodies piled in the road and then stopped his vehicle suddenly in a hiss of air brakes forcing those behind him to stop. The cheering faltered, gradually abated and then stopped. All the men in the advancing trucks had now seen and become aware of the small group of armed white men standing in front of the crest of the road facing them. They had expected to find that their fellow Simba had routed the Congolese Army, as usual, and had come out of town to take part in the celebration and looting. Instead they now had the bad luck to come across the first white mercenary Commando in the first action of the brand-new campaign meant to turn back the Simba advance. As the cheering stopped there was a long period of silence and inaction, but again time distorted and stood still.

Half of the Commando's men had gone forward by then and were still bunched on the narrow road, some sitting or kneeling so those behind could fire over them. Wilson, in the front row, took a step forward, spread his legs for balance, raised his rifle, lent into it and fired rapid booming shots at the silently staring men on the laden trucks. A firestorm erupted and the thunder of heavy automatic rifles was again deafening, as the smell of gun smoke rose strong and acrid in the humid air. Rebels on the two trucks fired a few shots in a panicked response but most tried to escape by jumping off and running back down the road. Those rebels who were smart and keen to live leapt for the cover of the undergrowth, and some of them might have escaped. There were very few of the men who had come forward on the trucks who lived through that merciless, meatgrinder of a firestorm. A score of self-loading heavy automatic assault rifles fire rapidly put down hundreds of rounds a minute.

My own first twenty-round magazine emptied in aimed shots at the running men. Aim, hold, fire as the rifle slammed my shoulder, held tight and steady. All around me were men shooting as fast as they could at the retreating rebels and my ears were almost deaf. As the breech of the rifle stayed open on the empty magazine a spare, charged one slammed home in a millisecond. Aim, hold, grip, fire and halfway down the magazine in that altered and suspended time. All around me and filling every sense, the insane thunder of rifles hammering. The edge of vision showed me some mercenaries firing on fully automatic, rifles in the shoulder and the muzzle arching skywards as a full magazine burst stuttered out, uncontrolled and a waste of ammunition, firing in fear at the vegetation alongside the road. Others fired and aimed but over-hasty shots meant that three or four rounds were needed to hit the target and then a quick switch to another running man and the same rapid fire. Living a lifetime inside a clap of tropical thunder, but there was no lightning, only curling smoke clouds.

The firing tapered off, became sporadic and stopped completely. There were no targets, real or imagined, left. That unearthly silence was only broken by the odd, faraway rifle shot from deep in the jungle. Shots that sounded like fire crackers and not of danger, cocooned as the shooters were by heavy vegetation. Those solitary little shots grew further and further away as the rebels, who were lucky enough to have escaped, ran for the safety of town. The heat of the rifle barrel warmed my hand as it gripped the stock, the steel barrel heating the wood. With only another two full magazines of rounds, forty spare and some in the rifle magazine, panic came again. When would the massed counterattack come? Would it be possible to nurse the ammunition and survive?

The horror of the preceding few minutes repeated in my mind: my rifle rear peep sight picking out a standing man and the trigger releasing, the slight mechanical rattle and slam of the gas piston reloading the chamber, the spent case is wheeling across my vision. The target smacked to the ground like a body falling from a height, bounce, bounce. The peep sight on a running man and as he entered a clearing in the trees, trigger, the rattle of the piston, a kick in the shoulder and the man slamming down, bounce, bounce. Was it really me causing that? Many times over a picked target was slammed down by other bullets, not mine, and a new one picked up in the sights. Bodies hanging thick from the truck side, piled on the road and along the jungle edges. There were bodies in piles slowly seeping black wet blood. Time had gone by without end while the blast of heavy rifles stung my ears and now the sudden utter silence.

With a sweep of his arm Wilson waved the Commando forward and the van reached the first pile of bodies. Some of those who still breathed were shot. That too was in panic, done in fear without any orders. What if the wounded suddenly, recovered, stood up and began shooting? The rebels in that first heap on the road were all half naked and carried a wide collection of weapons. The Simba had been gathered in the road by the local witchdoctor and magic water worked better on bare skin. Some had carried exquisitely made broad-blade spears which were at once collected as trophies. Some had carried bows, small bows almost like toys but with a quiver of poisoned arrows. There were many assorted rifles and sub-machine guns. One dead man had been carrying a FN and a webbing belt with spare magazines. I won the scramble and got to him first and made them mine. Blood was spreading darkly on the ground under the body. A treasure of six magazines came out of the webbing pouch draped round his neck which a quick check showed was full of gleaming brassy rounds. I was strong again and now invincible.

At the scene of the first contact with the medicine man and company, a fluttering vibration filled the air over the bodies, which were oozing dark blood from multiple gunshot wounds. Busy clouds of brilliant-coloured butterflies were whirling over the scene and dense concentrations of the insects sat sipping the oozing blood. The salts in the blood attracted them and the green flies. The butterflies always appeared in a very short time after blood was spilt in the tropical forests. The still moist air quickly took up and conveyed the smell of fresh blood. That cloying scent along with the sharper reek of cordite was filling my lungs as I watched the fluttering insects; they took me back to childhood, taking me back briefly to the happy hunting of the earlier days. Then it was back to here and now.

After the first pile of dead had been picked over for anything useful the men moved on towards the many other corpses piled up around and on the trucks, fifty metres further down the road. As we moved forward towards the killing ground there again came the sound of more trucks growling slowly through the jungle. The obvious conclusion was that those few Simba who had escaped from the first trucks had got back to town and now heavy reinforcements were on the way. The intensity of the sounds said there were many more trucks this time, a menacing, roaring growl echoing in the tall trees. The first vehicles had carried about fifty men, so maybe several hundred were on the way now. Some extra ammunition had been captured from the dead but the Commando did not have enough for a prolonged battle. There had been a lot of heavy firing, a lot of it pointless and now ammunition stocks were low. No-one wanted to go forward to meet a massed counterattack with low ammunition. Wilson ordered a retreat back to the transport and back to the village which we had left earlier that morning. Given the circumstances it was the only order that would have been obeyed. The retreat was disorderly and fast. Once you start running panic sets in.

If that action had come a few weeks later when we had been in the field longer there would have been several hundred more dead Simba that day. It later turned out the rebels in town heard the first and second actions and had piled onto trucks to go and loot the expected Congolese Army dead. Those Simba in town, when they heard the second battle assumed that another, bigger group of Congolese Army had been contacted after the first battle and as usual routed, so hundreds more took transport and left town to join the festivities. It was their lucky day. By the time the Simba reached the piles of their dead, which caused them to beat a terrified retreat, the Commando was doing the same in the other direction. Such confusion is the result of no military intelligence reports. It is also the result of the natural fear of death.

Later I tried to remember the number killed that morning. There were about thirty dead with the witchdoctor. They were all on the road in the open. The dead on or near the trucks, on the road next to them and in the immediate vicinity of the trucks visible in the undergrowth must have numbered about a hundred. There must have been scores more hidden in the jungle. Many more had been wounded but how many died from wounds was not possible to even guess. Being involved in that massacre meant I was responsible for the death of many men; how many was impossible to say.

If hundreds more rebels had been shot that morning it would have saved the lives of many who died at rebel hands later. But instead of advancing the Commando retreated in ignorance and fear and once started the retreat turned into a near rout. As the drivers and passengers in the vehicles began to imagine pursuit by thousands of vengeful rebels, the speed of the small convoy over the rough and wet track became faster and faster. Once started panic increased. Soon passengers were being bounced high and almost thrown out of our Jeep which several times narrowly missed skidding into trees. Eventually in a blind fear and rage I grabbed the driver by his hair and yanked his head back and threatened to put a bullet in him if he did not slow down and drive carefully. Boeta was on other transport and was no longer the driver. The other three men in the Jeep cheered. The Jeep slowed to a more careful pace, the driver now more scared of me than the demons chasing him.

Our Jeep got back to the village some time after the other vehicles and on arrival found the Commando had built the soon-to-become-familiar roadblock which was manned to repel the expected attack. Some rusted car bodies had been overturned in the road and whatever other suitable material that could found stacked up. Wilson looked crestfallen when no pursuit was reported, as the rear vehicle's report had been expected to give information on the size of the counterattack. The senior staff retired to drink tea with the missionaries and discuss the matter. The rest of the Commando searched for food and drank water from a roof tank at one of the houses. Some paw paws were found and shared. All the men were on edge and loud arguments broke out.

Sitting on the veranda of an abandoned house on a cane-weave chair my mind whirled. Other men milled about all in a state of high tension and talking loudly. So that was combat. Or was it? Shots had been fired at me with intent to kill. My own rifle had fired back, not me, the rifle. Aimed and fired and the target slammed down to the ground. Time and again a target in the ring of the rear peep sight and the rifle clacking and kicking to slam the target down. My ears still rang and my mind was dizzy trying to make sense of it all. Surely in combat the enemy inflicted casualties and some of your own men died? The one-sidedness of it all left a strong feeling of wrong in me. Was this the fruits of a Calvinistic upbringing or a sense of justice?

Boeta appeared with a wide grin on his face and sat down on a chair next to me.

"Fuck, that was good, Smiler. Stuck it to them good, hey? Saw you firing like you were on the range. Cool bloke, hey. See some of the other fuckers firing at stuff all on auto at that, spraying the bush. Some of these fuckers are a total waste of rations man. Hey, have you got ammo? Come. I've got a stash, come fill your magazines."

Just then Harry appeared and came over to us. "A bit of a balls-up, would you say? We shoot off one way and they squirt off north. Bets on that? Ah, well we are here to do as we are told." He stuck a match to his pipe and soon blue, fragrant smoke trickled from his nose.

"Boeta, this is Harry. Know him from pommy land. Me and Boeta know each other from hunting," I said.

They looked each other over. That tension-filled moment was when the three of us formed a mutual protection group. There was no agreement made, no handshake. There was only some affinity between us that we would have been hard put to explain. Other such small groups probably formed that day throughout the rest of the Commando, men with something in common aligning themselves to others like themselves. Death had reached out a cold hand and now was the time to unite to push that hand away.

"C'mon, let's load up with ammo and go out there to the road block. Maybe we will get lucky and the Simba attack. What you guys say?"

"Right on," Harry smiled round his pipe, "let's get out there and shoot Africa white."

"Well that's a better plan then fucking Africa white like the Portuguese want to."

There was no attack that afternoon but during the night an old VW Kombi was stopped by the outlying sentries near the roadblock. It was driven by a priest from the mission in Lisala who had come to find his fellow priests in this village to tell them the rebels had fled the town shortly after the battle that morning. He gave us information that the Simba, when news reached town, had commandeered every bit of transport they could find and had left so hastily on the road north that for many kilometres outside the town trucks were smashed against trees or stuck in mud wallows. When, the father wanted to know, would we be coming to secure the town we had taken? This first contact was a forerunner to the sort of war we now found ourselves in.

Since the stay at the comfortable hotel on the equator a reporter from the *New York Times* had been travelling with us. He was a heavy man with a black beard and thick glasses who carried a dozen cameras on slings round his shoulders. He rode with Wilson at the van of the convoy and at every stop ran about snapping pictures. He soon became an accepted part of the Commando, he blended in and no one paid him much attention. Each man was too busy with his own emotions to bother about a reporter. If it was a strange thing then so was everything else. The scene of the first contact he had recorded in detail with his cameras, using the time the dead were being looted in busily taking pictures. The retreat had been too fast to allow him to stop and use his camera. The next morning when the Commando eventually reached Lisala the reporter vanished at the airfield, flying out with the Americans.

Some weeks later a battered *Time* magazine arrived at our housing and on the front page was a photograph of 51 Commando busy picking over the piled up bodies. Photos of wounded being shot also featured inside. The cover headline read "Wilson and his Mad Dog Killers." There was no mention in the story that followed of the panicked retreat. The Commando delightedly pored over it, and burst out laughing as some of the hyperbole of the reporter was read out. If there ever was an aura of toughness connected to 'Congo mercenary', it was fabricated by reports such as that one. There were similar reports, in the same awed tones in other papers we saw, many times, during the Hoare days. The men involved loved to be personally identified in the reports; the same behaviour can be seen in at sports matches when the TV camera picks out someone in the crowd and inane waving and face-pulling follows. Most of the reports were so loaded with extra stuff that did not happen that it was hard to match the report to an actual event.

Belgian Congo askaris. (Wikicommons)

Moise Tshombe. (Wikicommons)

Patrice Lumumba. (Wikicommons)

Mercenary Mike Hoare in the Congo, 1964. (*Agence Presse*)

Two of Hoare's veterans. (Wikicommons)

A road patrol in the jungle outside Bumba. The author is driving, Barry is the gunner and Boeta is behind the driver. (Author's collection)

The 'mad dog killer' posse outside Lisala. The author is third from left. (Author's collection)

	STATEMENT OF SAVINGS ACCOUNT		
DATE	DEBIT	CREDIT	BALANCE
SEP 1-65			***1-0 CD
SEP 30-65	***5—0-0	**453-11-0	***454—8-0 ▷ HL
SEP 30-65			***449—8-0 AW HL
OCT-6-65	***5—0-0		***444—8-0
OCT-8-65	**250—8-0		***194-8-0 PA
OCT 15-65	***10—0-0		***184—8-0 UA
OCT 15-65	**35—0-0		***149—8-0 KA
OCT 20-65	***70—0-0		***79—8-0 CP XC
OCT 20-65	***35—0-0		***44—8-0 AW AC
NOV 11-65	***40—0-0		***4—8-0 CC
NOV 22-65		***7—4-0	***11-12-0
NOV 22-65	***4—0-0		***7-12-0

NOV 23-65	***5—0-0		****2-12-0 HA
NOV 30-65		**146—1-3	***148-13-3 ARSC OB
DEC-2-65	***45—8-0		***103-13-3 LE
DEC-2-65	***51—8-0		***52-13-3 SME
DEC 10-65	***20—8-0		***32-13-3 BK
DEC 15-65	***20—8-0		***12-13-3 LE
DEC 15-65	***10—0-0		***2-13-3 LE
JAN 10-66	***2-10-0		****—3-3 CO
APR 28-66		***45-15-5	***45-18-8 CO
APR 28-66	***30—8-0		***15-18-8 CO
MAY-4-66	**10—8-0		****5-18-8 AW DD

All entries in this pass-book must be made on the Society's machines. and no handwritten or other entries will be recognised.

The author's savings account book. (Author's collection)

Congolese Army victims. The author is on the right. Boeta (right) is about to knock down the shooter. (Author's collection)

This sequence of four photographs shows a mercenary executing a rebel. (Author's collection)

Colonel Jean Schramme (top left)with
a Katangese soldier (top right); the man
in the Jeep with a French Para badge is
a German mercenary. (Wikicommons)

A Commando recce unit advances on Baraka. Most were killed or wounded. (Wikicommons)

The dash to Baraka. (Wikicommons)

A mercenary officer directs a Katangese recoilless rifle team. (Wikicommons)

Flemish mercenary Marc Goosens discusses the next move with Taffy Williams and Armand Ianarelli. Within moments of this photo being taken, Goosens was dead. (Wikicommons)

GPMG gunner kitting up on the banks of the Congo River. (Wikicommons)

A gun jeep from the Schramme column. These fast, heavily-armed jeeps were the spearhead of many mercenary advances. (Wikicommons)

Classic engagement with gun jeeps. The lead jeep is a CJ6, the following a French Hotchkiss version of the old Willys. (Wikicommons)

6

So Lisala became the first town to be reclaimed, albeit messily, from the rebel advance. 51 Commando was the first Commando in the field but was soon followed by others. Apart from the abortive foray Hoare had attempted into the Great Lakes region there had been no previous contact between white mercenaries and the Simba rebels. As 51 Commando drove into town that day I still had no clear image in my mind of what a rebel looked like, what he wore or what weapons he carried. The previous day a large assortment of weapons ranging from barbed fishing spears to NATO-type MAGs in 7.62 calibres and belt-fed had been collected at the battle site. But the dead were also in a motley array of dress. Some were naked and some in ragged civilian clothes and a few in filthy army camouflage. The naked rebels had obviously been fed the age-old tale, stripped and sprinkled with magic water by the witchdoctor; they would be impervious to bullets and invisible. This shibboleth reared its ugly head in the 1800s in German East Africa, and has been used down the years by almost all soothsayers in the employ of African armies right to the present time. Even today in the Central African Republic of Congo one rebel faction calls itself the 'Mia Mia', meaning water, water.

As the Commando convoy first entered the town any person in sight became a target. With no clear image of the enemy fear made everyone the enemy. The assumption was that anyone still in town was the enemy. This turned out to be totally wrong, as all the rebels had beaten a hasty retreat the previous day while we were doing the same in the opposite direction. Luckily for them the few who had not fled into the jungle, and were hiding inside houses knew from bitter experience there would be indiscriminate shooting. Every time a town fell to the rebels or the government there was the same orgy of shooting. The learning curve for the Commando was steep but early that first day civilians thought to be rebels were shot at. Most of the shots were taken at long range and the targets were running hard so maybe none was killed. I used that thought as sop to my conscience. On the advance through town to the mission we did not stop to check the effect of our shooting.

The same priest who had called the previous night directed us to a massive church and outbuildings where his mission was still working. Silent white nuns and missionaries came out of the building to carefully greet us. The town was eerily quiet and the opinion of the men was that the rebel forces were gathering in the fetid rainforests surrounding the town and an attack in massed strength was imminent. Our dirty, unshaved and dangerous looking group were the first government agents the missionaries had seen since the rebellion began many months previously. They had been confined to the mission against their will by the rebels, but not physically harmed. The Commando took up positions in the multi-storey residential block near the church, once a boarding house for pupils at the mission school. There was a second floor balcony with a low stone wall at the edge and machine guns were set on the wall to cover the approaches. World War Two Mills bombs were put out and primed, ready to throw. In the first hour one of the drugged-up sentries accidentally fired his rifle and hit one of those grenades. It shattered without exploding.

This sort of dangerous carelessness was the signature of the type of men who served with me during that six-month contract. Few of the rank and file had military training, and no discipline was enforced. The sergeants and officers were barely better trained. The senior men, who had been picked for promotion on the information they gave while joining up, were comparatively better trained with military backgrounds, but they did not enforce discipline in the men. There was no loyalty in anyone to appeal to. The senior men had no law or military police to back them. Over the months several senior officers and NCOs were shot in the back during a firefight. Others were gunned down during drinking sessions when an argument broke out over orders given previously. There was no law; that was the first lesson to be learnt. Only the strong enforced their version of the law in this savage country.

It was clear from day one at Kamina there was no one to turn to for justice except your own friends. Fortunately Boeta counted me as a friend. Everyone had seen him gleefully rushing to be at the front and to get as near as possible to the enemy. Everyone had seen how much he enjoyed the fighting. The dead, wolf-like grey eyes chilled anyone they fell on. The other man of our group at the time, Harry, was a Canadian who smoked a pipe constantly and had big, sleepy brown eyes. He was an ex-Mountie and totally at ease when bullets flew. We had met briefly in a coffee shop in Copenhagen in another life. Then we had been deck hands on a Norwegian ship for a few days together. Harry travelled the world looking for excitement. That search for excitement was the basis of a bond between us. Harry and Boeta had the same wild adventurous spirits, only Harry was a total cynic. Both were physically strong. Three strong men standing together was enough insurance against even the most drunk and befuddled idiot. Three men watching each other's back made the wildest man think again.

That first day was waited out in a sweat of fear but the long-expected attack never came. The humid, steamy night drove me to seek sleep outside in the cooler air on the balcony. But even there it was too hot and humid to sleep under a blanket. The air was again so thick with mosquitoes that a hand waved made contact with a dozen of the insects that felt as big as wasps. Throughout the six months men went down with malaria. Luckily as the disease was so widespread and well known in the Congo it was possible to get the correct medicine from the missions. Mission stations were still working at odd places round the country, albeit in much reduced circumstance. They also carried penicillin, which treated those many mercenaries who needed to be cured of venereal disease. Many of the men who consorted with black women, who were available for very little money, were South Africans who came from a country where there was a strict prohibition of contact across the colour bar. Forbidden fruit is the sweetest?

That night on the balcony, lying on the concrete floor batting away the mosquitoes, the disturbing thoughts again hammered in my brain. For the past two days in any still moment my mind had been trying to cope with the tremendously disturbing, unnatural events. I had killed men; over and over my mind returned to that thought and shied away. It was me who had aimed and fired the rifle and men had fallen by the road, forest and trucks. Many had fallen and I had killed them. My belief had always been that killing a man would cause strong emotions. How many men had I killed? Why was there no remorse or regret? Why did I not have strong emotions?

My tired mind went back again and again to that morning two days ago. Aim, fire and men had fallen. But there was a raging storm of bullets as all around other rifles were thundering. There was the whiplash of incoming bullets. Aim, steady, fire, as drilled to do in the army. Lying there on the stone floor of the balcony, in a missionary building in the Congo night and itching from mosquito bites, my mind tried to grasp that momentous idea but kept shying away from it. There was no reaction, a blank calmness where there should have been some emotion. No remorse and no gladness, just emptiness. It had not been personal; was that why it meant nothing? It was war and they were trying to kill me? Restless sleep came without the questions being resolved. It is too terrible a thing to just ignore, my mind insisted but could not wrestle out a definite and final answer. How could it be that when men died by my hand it made no discernable impact? All my previous life experience had taught that killing another man was a serious thing, something that would bother me.

Killing? I was soon to learn that I knew virtually nothing of killing yet. On the morning of our second day in Lisala the Congolese Army came to town. A couple of hundred men in dirty green uniforms and heavily armed, arrived in an assorted convoy of commandeered, mostly civilian vehicles. The killing began as soon as they arrived on the outskirts of town. They hunted down anybody hiding in houses and shot them to death. The white priests and nuns retreated into the recesses of the building held by the mercenaries. They had lived through it all before. Each time control of the town changed hands the killing started again. The holy men refused to abandon their work and trusted in God and now the white mercenaries would protect them. It turned out that the local tribesmen thought of us as gods.

The local black population tried to run for cover in the crowding forest when the soldiers came to buildings in which they hid, seeking to rape, kill and loot, ran as best they could. And anyone who ran was shot at once. All the males who put up their hands were taken captive; females were raped then there in the street before being taken into captivity. The captive men were then marched at gunpoint to large pits dug by earlier captives and made to stand on the lip of the pit and then shot by several rifles, knocked off the lip of the pit to join the pile of bodies already rotting in the crater. Many male captives were first maliciously beaten to a pulp with rifle butts and then bayoneted at the mass grave instead of being shot. Anyone who lived in a town once held by rebels was guilty of being a rebel. The women were pushed into the houses the soldiers commandeered and abused day and night. That was the Congolese Army law. Likewise when the rebels took control of a town their law assumed that all were government agents and the same slaughter took place. All day and night gunfire rattled and screams of tortured men and women filled the air around the Commando holed up in the mission building.

The rape and murder went on day after day and all night as well. Time was in suspense and distorted as in a dream; it might have been a long or short time. The rich cloying smell of blood and rotting flesh hung heavy in the air. The corpses of those shot while running away lay where they fell in the streets and backyards, bloated with gas and fast rotting in the humid air. Gleaming white skeletons of victims of the previous period of Simba rebel rule were to be seen all over town and now new bones were being added to the litter. The mayhem slowed when the Army could find no more people to butcher, but raping of the unfortunate females continued day and night. The screaming never stopped. The last and only survivors of the townspeople were those who had taken to the jungle. That dense sea of green pressed close to the outer buildings of the town; it seemed to me to be a crouching beast waiting to attack the puny man-made buildings. No mind could take it all in and stay sane while understanding the scale of the killing and most of it was screened out by self-protective filters, dimmed now by the curtain of time. Like turning your eyes away from an ugly sight, so my mind shies away from those half-remembered massacres.

The consensus was that the mayhem was not our business. The Congolese Army were authority and it was their country. There was no way for us at that brutal time to know for sure who was selected for execution and no way of knowing if it was justified. The desperate screams of women being raped came from afar for days on end. Again it was not our business or our country. None of us was going to risk life to intervene on behalf of unknown women. It would have been different if they had come for the white missionaries. That would have been our business, but the Army knew that, knew we would not allow it. In the end the missionaries pleaded with Wilson to stop the wanton mayhem and he agreed and went off to talk to the Congolese commander. He may have been successful as a day or so later the shooting and beatings began to abate, battered woman were pushed out of buildings by soldiers, sent on their way and some days later residents fearfully crept out from the jungle and tested the streets.

In Africa the dead are buried with ceremony by relatives. The number of corpses left to rot where they died at that time was the result of the massive disruption of family life by the mass killings. It must have happened many times that entire families died. The rebel dead would have come from far-off tribal lands and there would be no relatives nearby to bury them. The army dead, those killed by the attacking rebels, were abandoned in retreat by the flight of fellow soldiers. Sometimes the bodies were cut up for black magic medicine. The dead and abandoned government troops were usually from a distant tribal district and were also left where they fell. The mass graves, eventually filled in by soldiers, were not opened to recover relatives for burial. Some dead who had nearby relatives were moved away secretly at night from the streets. Any mercenary dead, who were fortunately few, where buried when time permitted if the bodies could not be flown out of the country. Burial of the dead was not something that was discussed in advance or planned for. Everyone was convinced he was immortal. A belief in immortality is required of any soldier. The rites we practise for the dead are for the comfort of the living.

The men of the Commando were in the grip of fear in those terrible few days and dreaded the thought of leaving the relative safety of the building. Going out to where an attack could be launched on us by surprise occupied most minds. We were still raw and new in the field and fear was the motivation for most of our actions. Boeta was alone in agitating for action, any action. Two of the mass graves were within sight of the fortified balcony and the daily mass murders could be both seen and heard. The slayings further away could also on occasion be seen; that alone stoked the fear. The expectation of a mass counterattack made it seem prudent to stay in a fort as we were few and they would be many. Ignorance always breeds fear. Our fear forbade help for the dying, and kept us locked in safety.

Time slipped by and it became obvious that no attack from the rebels was going to be mounted, making it feel relatively safe to venture out of the fortified building. It was at that time that Wilson told the sergeants to try and stop further killing by the Army. We were all sickened and angered by the orgy of needless death. Patrols of mercenaries on Jeeps set out to roam the streets of the town. Once out and about it was easier to grasp of the situation as sitting waiting indoors had isolated us from the real situation on the ground. The feeling once outside, exposed as we were in the Jeeps, was totally different to that when inside. We had been bound by fear. As usual Boeta was the first to go out and made the rest of us follow his lead.

"What you say, Smiler," Boeta asked impatiently as he had done many times before. He was looking down at the town from the balcony. Distant shots still echoed in the streets."Time to get out there a shoot a few bastards?"

"And then?" asked Harry talking round his pipe, "When we have shot them all, then what? Or you going to leave a few to mow the lawn? Do the washing and cleaning?"

"Come guys, let's get out there," Boeta said, shrugging on his ammunition belt. "Some blacks may be good ones. The bastards might kill some good blacks. But then the only good black is a dead one, hey."

"Sounds like an idea," I agreed, a tinge of excitement rising, "but I want to drive. OK?"

"Suits me fine, want both hands free. Harry, you do the Browning?"

"Don't know why I listen to you mad fuckers. C'mon, let's go out and commit suicide." His pipe puffed like a miniature train.

My choice to drive was as a result of the dangerous headlong flight over dreadful roads a few days earlier. After that it was my firm intention to drive the vehicle I travelled in at all times, as was necessary for self-preservation. Anyway the front seat was padded and the most comfortable. On that first tentative patrol in Lisala there was only Harry and Boeta with me in the Jeep. Other vehicles also cautiously went out with a few men after us but many others still chose to wait and see from the relative safety of the mission. Boeta spoke a bit of Swahili, and Harry spoke French so they were able to communicate with the few frightened locals whom we met on the streets. Within half an hour it was obvious that the mercenaries were in fact in full control of the town and the hidden dangers and ambushes were imaginary.

"Take those bastards," Boeta, who was sitting behind me, shouted in my ear. He pointed to a group of four bedraggled soldiers prodding two thin men dressed in the ragged remains of shirt and trousers along with rifles towards a still uncovered execution pit. The abject men must have been captured some time previously elsewhere in the town. Did the soldiers not know that the order had been given to stop killing?

"Stop!" Boeta shouted as we came to a halt. He stood up in the back of the Jeep and his rifle was held by the pistol grip, barrel pointing at the sky, the butt in his waist. With his left hand he pointed at the suddenly startled soldiers. "You there, bring those two men here." He spoke Swahili loudly.

"Ja, right on." Harry muttered to me. Then he pulled the machine gun down from pointing up at the sky and swung the shielded gun around to cover the small group. "Release those men," he shouted in French.

The dirty soldiers look around, turning left and right, feigning surprise. Then one pointed at himself and asked in French. "Are you talking to us?"

"Listen donkey cock, run away, run away fast, and you will live another day," Boeta shouted in Swahili. The bolt of his rifle clacked loudly as he cocked and released it.

"We apologise sir, we are going now sir," called the same man in French.

The soldiers quickly laid the rifles they carried down on the pavement and trotted away down the road with their hands above their heads.

"Sir, sir, can I shoot a couple, please sir," Harry intoned. But we let them go.

The few vehicle patrols that day stopped other parties on the way to the execution pits and saved lives. Armed mercenaries in a Jeep with a machine gun were very intimidating to the armed thugs intent on the execution of unarmed men; thugs who were engaged in boosting their own sense of manhood. Rescued prisoners were taken to the mission where they were left in the care of the fathers until it was safe for them to leave. Within hours of the mercenaries taking action the word had spread. Murder of civilians ceased. That day we finally learnt the Congolese Army was in dreadful, awed fear of the mercenaries. Word had been spread about, rumours of white giants with big beards carrying machine guns in each hand, giants from whose skin bullets ricocheted as if they were made of rock. Mercenaries were abroad and they were angry.

The fear of black magic played a big part in the lives of the tribesmen who lived in those rainforests. When the rebels phoned ahead to the garrison of the town they were advancing on, the fear of black magic came into play. When word was sent that the witch-doctor with the rebels had given them powerful medicine, the fear of black magic was such that in a few short hours the Congolese Army deserted the town. In their headlong flight the retreating army left visible spells of their own to discourage pursuit. Some spells took the form of a pig or a monkey being impaled up the anus by a spear and planted in the middle of the road, with trinkets and bits of human skin draped over the symbol to make it stronger. The side with the best-known and most respected witch-doctor was the most powerful in battle. This belief in the supernatural is embedded in the African. The old savage kings had controlled their subjects by using witchdoctors and holding sniffing-out ceremonies. Even in modern Africa spells are often still used. Think of the recent media reports of chickens and black cats killed in the stands by football teams seeking to hex rivals.

Once order had been restored, and the reality that we were the ruling kings grasped, the Commando set out to see if there was anything left to loot. The shops were long empty, but the odd sturdy safe was found yet opened. The post office safe seemed intact and the bank-vault type door had only been damaged but not opened. Our little party spent several hours working on that post office vault door. A long, heavy chain from the dock on the Congo River and a big truck found still in working order were used in an attempt to haul away the steel door. It was decided a running jerk was needed and the truck was reversed to the wall and then gunned away at full revs. The truck's back axlel and wheels broke away when the chain snapped tight. Harry then stepped up to the plate with a bazooka, the American-made anti-tank rocket launcher. Three screeching rounds later the door came away and we rushed inside. The entire wall at the back of the vault, the side opposite the vault door, was missing. We were too late and the shelves were bare, cleaned out by whoever had smashed down the back wall.

Another safe was found and dug out of a wall with crowbars. The heavy safe had been in a warehouse on the riverbank near the docks so was carried out to the strong, wooden-pile dock. Boeta had some plastic explosive and the safe was placed carefully over the explosive.

"Stop laughing Smiler, I know what to do, I've often done it," Boeta said.

"Hope you have mate, because it looks bloody funny to me," Harry intoned.

"No look, it's a shaped charge and that will cut open the safe door. No problemo."

"Don't think so Boeta, but try anyway" I said.

On the mines part of my job had been to take misfired explosives to a nearby quarry and blow them up and so explosives were not a mystery to me. This one was not going to work. I could see that, but was interested to see what would actually happen.

"Right on, going to do just that. No doubt you guys will want some of the loot so stop smiling like that."

The safe was the size of a small refrigerator and two blocks of explosive, maybe one kilogram of it, was under the safe which was lying face down on its door. Boeta put in detonators and reeled out a wire to the corner of the building and fired the charge with an electric detonator and battery. After the explosion there was just enough time to see the safe arc through the air and hit the river two hundred metres from the dock. After we stopped laughing we went on looking for money. But after an extended search, when no money was found, the never-ending search for food began. The unit had been making do on what had been transported from the equator hotel. The only food left was Belgian Army ration packs obtained from the Congolese Army barracks when their transport had been commandeered. Those packs had almost run out, and the senior men were keeping what was left over for themselves. Bananas were plentiful and alongside the roads the odd pineapple was the food most easily found and often the only food to be had.

Searching for something to eat took up a lot of each day throughout the contract. Arms, ammunition and transport were scarce, but could usually be raised. Food, however, was much harder to find. The local tribesmen were living on what they could scrounge from the jungle and river and had nothing to spare. Even the Congolese Army could not bludgeon food out of the locals. Foraging along tracks into the jungle outside of town yielded bananas, mainly the plantain variety which the locals dried to flour, and pineapples which grew in the village clearings. At times a stray chicken got unlucky but most village poultry were savvy and impossible to catch. Shooting a scrawny, fast-running bird left little meat to eat. Eventually a local street market came about but even there the only food was eggs, palm oil and spices. Tropical jungle is not very productive of animals as trees with edible fruit are widely scattered. Tropical jungle is the same environment as a desert for mammals. Boeta and I both knew that so did not attempt to hunt for meat. It would have been a long and possibly useless hunt.

During that time of almost constant hunger a small miracle happened. A South African women's service group had put together a large shipment of food and sent it off to darkest Africa for the mainly South African mercenaries of 5 Commando Group. Most of the donation had vanished along the way, as would be expected. One afternoon a battered river steamer called at the Lisala docks and word reached 51 Commando that a shipment of food was on board the riverboat for them. It was hard to believe that anything could have been delivered from so far in those chaotic times.

The riverboats that had long plied the mighty river since the early Belgian days were of one design and had a double row of cabins above deck and a balcony running round the second level. As it was only a few years since the Belgians had left the country that boat was still in reasonable order and the captain and crew still in smart, if grubby, naval-type uniforms. Those riverboatss ran for decades as the main trade artery of the country and only today are finally falling apart. The captain welcomed us aboard and laid on a very good meal in the dining room. Afterwards carton after carton of frozen meat, rump and fillet steak, were unloaded and put on the Commando trucks and Jeeps. The miracle of that shipment was that it had made it all the way up the river; it was a journey of at least two weeks upriver from Leopoldville and the airport. The shipment had to survive the attentions of many hungry mouths between the airport and the river and again all that distance and time on the boat. For a week or more prime beef was the only item on the menu, three meals a day. When finally the never-ending search for food had to begin again it was a sad day for us all.

I had been wearing the same pair of camouflage trousers for weeks, since Kamina in fact, and they were stiff and black with encrusted dirt, body oils and sweat. There was an ornate water fountain at the mission and one afternoon the trousers were finally washed there. There was no soap available so it was really just a rinse and not a lot of dirt came off. With a towel round my waist I went off a short distance to sit in the sun and wait for the trousers to dry, but on my return they had been stolen. Boeta had a small stock of spare uniforms and he laughed at my rage and gave me another pair of trousers. I did not think it was wise to ask where they came from, in case they were from a dead man. But there was no chance of being squeamish and it was an immense relief to put on those pants. Having to walk around without was not nice. What type of man steals a fellow soldier's pants and a filthy pair at that?

"Pity you don't have crabs," Harry said, pipe in his front teeth and grinning.

"Total wastes of oxygen some of these fuckers. Come. Smiler, let's go and find the fucker. Make him pay." Boeta pulled his pistol out and checked the loading of the magazine.

"Na, leave it. If the sod is that desperate he can have them. These are a lot cleaner anyway."

After some time at the mission the Commando moved residence to the local boarding school hostel. It was a large red face-brick multi-storey building with many bedrooms, plenty of toilets and showers and a large kitchen. It was always surprising to find that the electricity and water still worked. The missionaries were responsible for that; most of them were artisans of one sort or another. It was at that school where our work for pay really began. So far it had been all unexpected crisis and now the routine would begin. Wilson decided the roads out of town were to be cleared of enemy. Each day vehicle patrols would go a bit further until the Commando could move on up the river towards the next town, Bumba, without opposition. Sections of four men to a Jeep were formed and two Jeeps would patrol together. The Jeeps were still the old US Army issue and a machine gun had been mounted on each.

The mission workshop was used to weld the modifications and soon each Jeep had a mounted machine gun firing over the front bonnet and protected by a bullet-proof shield. Each Jeep carried a .30 calibre Browning or a 7.62 NATO MAG, both belt-fed guns. Normally belts were hand-fed into a firing gun by an assistant. That meant two men to one machine gun. The modification we made added a cage fixed to the steel pole carrying the gun into which the ammunition belt box was put. With the box swivelling with the gun manual feeding was no longer needed so one man could fire the gun.

Each of the Jeep crew carried FN 7.62 assault rifles and handguns. As there was no webbing issued each man devised his own way of carrying any spare rifle magazines. The webbing was mostly taken from Simba dead, and preferred items were old British Army issue, probably originating from the time Uganda was part of the British Empire. A lot of rebels were from the north of the country, bordering Uganda. Spare ammunition in wooden crates was carried in the vehicles for both the machine guns and rifles. Side arm ammunition was the concern of the individual. As 9mm ammunition was plentiful a lot of the sidearms were that calibre.

In the time of the mass killings in Lisala Boeta had saved a thin, wiry local man from execution. They took a liking to each other and the rescued man stayed with us to the end of my contract. He was named Matahari and was used as a spy. He was also used as a translator, but mainly as an advanced spy sent forward on foot through the jungle to check out the next unknown jungle village. He became a rich man by constantly sending trucks loaded with looted goods to his village. At the end of our first contract, from Stanleyville, he sent home a convoy of six trucks loaded with dress material. He eventually became a respected storekeeper in his home village. Matahari proved to be very useful in the new task of road clearing. Sent ahead, he questioned locals and then returned on foot and passed information on to Boeta in Swahili. Our two-Jeep unit learnt a lot more of what was going on in the area with his help than we would have known without him. Local knowledge is always useful if strangers want to understand what is going on. After all, knowledge is power.

The lives of many innocent tribesmen were saved by Matahari. At first, before he came with the patrols, there had been a policy on road-clearing patrols to shoot anyone on sight as the risk of ambush was constantly there. Our patrol now stopped and sent him ahead when approaching a village clearing to speak to those living there. Matahari, a native of these forests, could tell at once who rebel supporters were or were not, simply by the way they reacted to him. He soon told to us that very few of the locals had joined or helped the rebels and in fact most local tribesmen were loyal only to the local chief and headman. Most of them had only a very vague idea of what or who government was as that agency was very remote from their lives. The tribesman's grasp of rebellion was hazy; rebellion against your own headman or chief was unheard of, and would make you a total outcast here in the jungle.

A routine was set. We went out each morning on the Jeeps to drive down the wet, muddy tracks looking for enemy. The enemy often obliged by waiting in ambush so the first we knew about them was when bullets cracked and swished through the air or a hand grenade exploded on the muddy road nearby. Then all guns would pour such a storm of rapid fire in the general direction of the hostile fire that leaves and branches rained down. A deep and sudden silence would fall, broken only by the murmur of the idling engines. No member of the patrol went off the road to check an ambush site, so we seldom knew how many had been killed. It was inconceivable that anyone could survive the bullet storm, and confirmation of that was the silence of the ambushers.

Our small convoys driving daily out of Lisala were lucky and almost always returned unscathed from ambushes set by the roadsides. It was not unusual to be fired at five or six times on a single patrol. The enemy were not as lucky. The patrol fire was very dense and deadly and the jungle offered only protection from sight and not from bullets. Numerous times an ambusher would stagger wounded out of the jungle and die on the road. The patrol always kept on firing till the enemy return fire was totally stopped. We also used fragmentation and phosphorus grenades, the latter at times igniting the vegetation. At rare intervals a vehicle took a hit or a man was slightly wounded. The enemy were careful to hide themselves in the dense forest at the roadside, shielded by vegetation so their total casualties were unknown. They died in big numbers and the stench of rotting flesh marked where previous ambushes had been. Our most seriously wounded, requiring more than a bandage, were flown out to eventually end up in a South African military hospital. We suffered few casualties.

Today when I think back on those days only cameo images remain in my memory. Long days melded into fleeting images, and not one day or the other sticks out. Probably the tension and fear it caused is the reason details of each patrol are hard to recount. Each morning was the same: first the search for food and making sure the weapons and ammunition were in order. Then that terrible, fearful excitement of impending doom as the Jeep engine started up. Mile after mile down the dank dangerous tunnels of the forest followed. The whiplash of incoming fire at regular intervals and the mind-numbing, ear-ringing roar of the return fire rattling your head.

When it was over and we drove on, through the stench of death, we saw the bodies at the edge of the road all chewed to bits and bleeding still and the gargling, coughing sounds of others dying unseen in the undergrowth. Then always the fluttering butterflies wheeling in to suck the black blood. We had songs we sang to give each other courage. I still hear sometimes eight male voices in chorus intoning, "Where have all rebels gone, long time passing. Fucked off every one, long time passing," and several other homemade verses. When we knew there was a definite ambush ahead the stick intoned, "This-will-be-the-longest-day, the longest day." The smell of rum and maple tobacco, and the cold glint of wolf eyes also punctuate my memories of those patrols as Harry and Boeta were always on the same Jeep. As well as the equator heat and rain and mud everywhere.

7

Ian was a slim, tall and shy, a man in his forties, with freckles, large ears and quietly spoken. He registered pained disapproval when the non-stop drinking and drug-smoking went on near him. We talked sometimes in the quiet of night when he told me some of his problems. His life had not been easy, and he had bad luck a lot of the time; some lives are like that. He had married young and now had six children of varying ages. It seems to me that poor men have lots of children; which is the cause and which the effect? He had recently been made redundant when the mine he worked for ran out of payable ore, so he joined up. Like all the rest of us it was the money. He desperately needed the money to feed his large family; the promise of a large salary had lured him, as it had us all. Just one contract would tide him over to another job. He was a qualified plumber and was sure he would be able to find a job again in a few months at the most. The money as a soldier of fortune would take good care of his family for some months until the job came. Most were in it for extra money but for Ian the money was a primal need; for others it was just a lust. If there were any men who had joined up just for the danger and excitement, they kept quiet about it and I never met them. Maybe it was inevitable that Ian would be the first to die.

The routine of patrolling out of the school had been in place for many days. Every morning the two sections of two Jeeps, four men in each, left after a scratch meal, each taking one of the tracks going north up the river. The distance travelled from Lisala extended each day. Theory had it that once a stretch of track had been cleared of ambushes it was completely clear of rebels. This premise was one hatched by Wilson and his senior staff. But as is usual in the military the senior staff did not go into action and Wilson and company did not move from the vicinity of the school. There was no debriefing of the men when they returned from patrol, and no contact with our headquarters at the school. It goes without saying that the same spot on the track, or a nearby previous contact site, was ambushed several times. Such is the nature of all military officers: in war time they give orders but do not take much part in action so can only guess about actual conditions. The onus at Lisala fell on each two-Jeep unit, and certainly on the individual, to do what they could to look after themselves but using common sense.

Once, at the very start of the road-clearing patrols, orders were given to take black soldiers of the Congolese Army with us, on the presumption they would know the area and be a help so three joined our two Jeeps one morning. A clearing in the jungle where a village stood alongside the road was reached about two kilometres out of town. Our section had several times been through the village with no problems and that day stopped to see if the local inhabitants had food to sell. As the patrol had already stopped to ask for food a few times previously the local tribesmen were no longer afraid. On that humid morning a group of villagers approached the Jeeps and without warning the black soldiers opened fire on them with bursts of automatic fire from sub-machine guns. It was sudden and shocking. Fortunately their aim was poor, which was worsened as their weapons, firing on automatic, kicked the gun muzzles up to the sky. The few other locals in the background ran like gazelles for the cover of the forest and a sickening anger raged through me at the stupidity of the black soldiers.

One tribesman, who had been shot through the stomach, was laid face down, pushing up on his hands and looking up with a shocked face. Another lay sprawled on his back, dead. Boeta had his face screwed to a pout that normally portended death for someone. In a towering rage he knocked the three soldiers down one after another with the butt of his rifle. Then he stood over the suddenly terrified men, making ready to shoot them. The soldiers were in a state of confusion and had no idea what they had done wrong.

"Wait, Boeta, wait." I advised him and pushed his rifle barrel up. "They come from a unit with a big cheese. No, wait; we could be arrested by the general."

"Shooting them could be a problem. Think, Boeta," Harry added his voice. "They could take a bullet if we hit an ambush later, you know."

"Shoot the bastards now. Fuck them."

"Rather take them in under arrest. Maybe the general will have them shot."

"Or shoot them in the next ambush."

"Fuck it. Do what you like." Boeta spat and then turned away, his face stilled screwed in an intense frown of deadly anger.

The reaction from the general who had come up with the Congolese Army to Lisala could not be predicted; armed confrontation with a unit that outnumbered the Commando by at least ten to one would not be pleasant. To kill the murderers could cause that confrontation. The hurt man was given a packet of cigarettes. His spine was affected and the bullets had cut open his stomach. Black blood oozed from under him and the butterflies were soon gathering in a scattered cloud. There was no medical help to give and nothing further could be done. The murderous soldiers were trussed tightly with wire from a nearby fence, tossed on to the Jeep and the unit returned to town. Before leaving we lit a cigarette for the injured man and the rest was up to his relatives, who were still hiding in the nearby forest. With no medicine or any doctor the wounded man could not have lasted long. Dying of a stomach wound is painful in the extreme, especially without medication. My emotion was of utter and pained hopelessness.

The black soldiers, now grey-skinned with terror, bound tightly and with their wrists bleeding, were taken back to Lisala to their unit quarters. As they were tossed off the trucks Boeta let loose a long and loud tirade in Swahili at the senior officer who came out of the building to see what the commotion was. The officer dragged the trussed men inside the house by their legs. He too was scared and shaking visibly as Boeta continued to rant and he loudly agreed with what was being said. The officer promised Boeta that punishment would be meted out, but could not hide the fact that he was wondering what all the fuss was about. Above the fright there was a puzzled look on his face. Why was there so much concern with the shooting of a few locals?

"Should have shot the fuckers," Boeta fumed. "Nothing will be done by that stupid bastard."

"What's the difference my friend, a couple more dead. What difference does it make?" Harry said and calmly lit his pipe and the rich scent of tobacco drifted.

"Look, man, they have armoured vehicles and there are hundreds of them, they come out after us someone's going to die. I don't want to die, do you?" I was scared that Boeta would provoke the officer into an attack on our small group; men were beginning to gather from inside the building, and a mob is not rational.

"Your trouble, Smiler, is you worry too much." Boeta turned the grey eyes on me and then gave a thin smile. "Fuck it all, you're right. Come on, let's go out again and see if we can find Simba to shoot."

No further patrols went out with components of the Congolese Army after that incident; not while the Commando was in the field on its own and without other units of 5 Commando Group. When the Commando eventually moved on to the next town the Congolese soldiers trailed behind two days later. Much later, when joined with other Commandos in the field, some black soldiers were added to the convoys. The men of 51 Commando were relatively ill disciplined and untrained, but the black soldiers were in league of their own when it came to disobedience. Ian was on the patrol that day and the death of those unknown tribesmen troubled him. Men who have seen a lot of grief in life always feel bad when other men suffer.

Later that day the little convoy of two Jeeps went out again, this time along a different track. Going north and still going upstream towards Stanleyville. That city was touted by everyone as the ultimate destination of the entire campaign. 51 Commando's efforts were wholly directed at getting to Stanleyville and attacking the city. Once that town was retaken, it was thought that the rebellion would end. There were still many hundreds of kilometres of jungle between us and that city. It was strange that those in charge believed taking a city would finish the rebellion. The cities were mere dots in the vast oceans of forest and savannah which make up the country. Stanleyville was the second largest city in the Congo, but it was still only a minor enclave in the vast areas of sparsely populated countryside. There is always little communication between city dwellers and isolated rural communities and in the chaos of the Congo at that time there was probably no communication at all. To this day the rulers in the Congo know nothing of the remote places in the country. There the tribal chiefs and warlords still rule.

Ian always wore Second World War British webbing, the sort with straps over each shoulder, on which were pouches that carried spare ammunition each side of the chest. A light coloured beret was always correctly cocked over his right eye. He normally sat behind the front left seat of the leading Jeep, always alert and awake. That day I was, as usual, driving the second of the Jeeps. Harry was in the other front seat behind the machine gun. Boeta and another sat in the rear on the hard wheel arches. There were four men in the front Jeep, eight of us in all. The weapons the unit carried could put down hundreds of rounds a second when fired in unison. The firepower of our unit was equal to that of a company of men from the great wars of Europe just decades back. That firepower was certainly what kept us alive through all the ambushes brushed off around Lisala.

The road was fairly good as, for once, it was dry. The midday heat was silent but for the hum of the engines. The heat and humidity were astonishing and so a slight haze of dust rose from the front Jeep. Gunshots rattled and bullets cracked through the heavy air, rude and loud. Ian stood up in the moving vehicle and began to bring his FN to bear on the ambush ahead of the lead Jeep and then he fell off over the side and lay still. There was a brief, vicious firefight. The thunderous storm of machine guns and automatic rifles filled all of my senses. The front Jeep reversed twenty metres to where our Jeep stood. Harry had opened fire with our .30 Browning, long bursts, and the rest of the riflemen stood and fired at the jungle ahead and alongside the road. When there was no return fire heard the weapons abruptly fell quiet. Ian lay where he had fallen without moving. Someone on the front Jeep shouted that there was a crossroad ahead, and that the ambush had come from the right-hand side road from a couple of huts.

The men opted to pull out as fast as possible and leave the body where it lay in the road. That one of our own was dead was shocking. Ian was the first casualty, causing awful reality to finally hit home. Death had been long anticipated and now it was here. Boeta and I quickly agreed the body had to be taken back or it would be hacked apart for black magic medicine and neither of us would allow that. Harry agreed to go along with us as well. The other man in the Jeep with us that day was Tom, a hairdresser and undertaker. He was thin and tall, always amused, always in good spirits. He was hard to know because he fended off all questions with jokes. Now he just smiled thinly and nodded his head. We drove forward and around the other Jeep, two rifles and the machine gun raked the jungle on both sides with rapid fire until the body was next to the Jeep. With my nerves screaming, I put down my rifle and jumped out. Boeta did the same. The limp body was lifted with difficulty to the open back of the Jeep. It felt very hot where my hands touched bare skin. Harry had taken the wheel and, as we leapt in, he reversed at speed while Tom fired long bursts with the Browning to cover the retreat. There had been no further firing by the hidden enemy after the first short burst that had killed Ian. A very subdued group arrived back at the mission school later that afternoon with the unit's first dead.

The nuns took over the body, laying it out in the church after it had been cleaned up. That they did so was an immense relief to all of us as only Tom had any idea what to do with a dead body. He, however, declined to get involved; instead he just smiled it off. The corpse was put in a coffin and then laid out in the church for last respects to be paid; it was there for two days. Harry was fascinated by the fact the corpse's beard grew and black stubble appeared on the chin. The burial was done in the church cemetery with full ceremony, priest and nuns in full regalia. This first casualty was probably the only mercenary to get a decent funeral. In the future some of the dead were buried in shallow holes quickly dug where they fell. The luckier ones were shipped home in body bags on an American freight plane, if they were lucky enough to die where it could be done. Ian's family never received his pay or insurance payout. This fact was only learnt months later and by then the struggle for everyone else's pay had been so long and difficult that there was no one to take Ian's side.

It has always been my belief that burial rituals are slightly ridiculous and a product of superstition. Church rites are all the same: superstitious mumbo-jumbo. The burial ceremony is of no interest to the dead person, although the ceremony focuses on the dead person as if he was present. Not many people see it that way, but the burial ceremony and the all that goes with it is today solely for the benefit of the living. Tom, the undertaker, agreed with my views when I shared them with him. But he was happy to make money out of foolish rites.

The constant and unending danger of the previous weeks had an unexpected effect on us all. Now if there was no immediate danger a listless boredom set in, often within an hour of being out of danger. The constant adrenaline feeding into the body when in mortal danger is just as much a habit-forming drug as any. After a day of constant vigilance and several firefights it was strange and disturbing to come back to the safety and quiet of the residential block. Suddenly there was no threat, no danger, and so the chemical load in the body fell. Sitting still and quiet felt very uncomfortable. It was then men used liquor and other drugs to replace the ebbing high of adrenaline and supreme boredom. It is strange how the human body can adapt to virtually any condition. The craving in the mornings to get out of town and look for a firefight began to motivate most of us, made us eager, and like addicts craving a fix we wanted our adrenaline.

This hunger for danger led our small unit into undertaking a task at the request of a missionary from a church centre about ten kilometres south of the town. The priest, dressed in his white clean cassock, had come to request help from the mercenaries. People at his church had reported Simba rebels hiding out in a disused used animal-pen complex near the massive stone church. The Simba had fled the missionary complex at the time of the mercenary advance on Lisala, but it now appeared some of them had merely taken to the nearby jungle and at night returned.

"Man, do you have to jump at all these dangerous jobs?" Harry smiled his sleepy smile at Boeta.

"Teach the bastards a lesson, fucking with the whites again." Boeta answered already alive and alert before it began.

"Death wish is what you got. Don't know why I come with you," I said.

"Because you fuckers like it as much as me."

After clearing an ambush a few days back a German Luger pistol had fallen into my hands, which had been swapped for an American AR 15, one of the latest rifles in use by Marines. The AR 15 had been traded for a drum-fed Thompson sub-machine gun, *à la* 1930s American gangsters, in .45 calibre. The Tommy gun was used by me for a short time but turned out to be too heavy and ammunition hard to get, so my FN 7.62 came back into favour and remained so for the rest of the contract. That day I carried the Tommy gun. The three of us set out in the Jeep with the priest. The mounted Browning had been taken off and as additional disguise we all wore white cassocks. The rebels could be alerted to the fact that mercenaries were at the church and as such they might then vanish only to reappear later and attack the white fathers in retaliation for having been reported. All of them had to be killed.

We were astounded by the mission. On the banks of the wide river stood a massive cathedral, something from the days of the European kings, grey stone walls seeming to float against the black river and blue sky. A bit of eighteenth-century Europe had been transported to tropical jungle. Some hectares of that jungle had been cleared of all undergrowth and only tall forest trees and old, equally tall palm trees left standing around the massive building. The area under the park-like trees was emerald green with planted grass lawns where benches were placed in shady spots. The manse and attending buildings near the church were also shaded under the trees, the sun dappled on the stone walls. The animal sheds stood some distance away at the edge of the lawn area and partly in the encroaching jungle. Going inside was difficult, as the weapons had to be carried concealed under our cassocks. Silent tribesmen watched from the distance; we fooled no one, but hoped they were loyal to the missionaries.

A meal of Nile perch steaks and mashed potatoes was served as night fell. That meal was certainly the equivalent of one served in mediaeval times to royalty when compared to the meagre rations we were used to. The noise of men eating with gusto went on for a long time much to the amusement of the ruddy-faced priest. Eventually the job on hand could not be put off for yet another serving. The three of us stood up burping and made ready. In addition to guns, we each carried a pistol in a holster. Then we had four grenades each, and Harry carried a Very flare pistol in case light was needed.

The trip in the dark to the animal sheds was fairly easy, and was done quietly through the park-like grounds. Each animal shed was checked with care and at the approach to the third one noise was heard inside. We stood dead still for a moment, listening to the muffled foot falls and clanking sounds, as something hard connected with wood. The animal shed door was missing. A grenade from each of us went in the open door and after the booming explosions we all opened up on full automatic fire into the shed from the doorway. As we stepped back to change magazines, there was absolute silence and not another sound could to be heard inside the shed over the ringing in our ears. We threw one more grenade to make sure and then Harry fired a Very flare into the pen that lit the room in crimson light. Lying in one corner was the mangled body of a goat. The church had a herd of milk goats but the rebels had killed them for meat. It soon emerged that one ram had escaped slaughter and went into the jungle verge and had taken to returning to the shelter of the stall at night.

After another royal meal for breakfast we reluctantly took the road back to Lisala without the cassocks.

"Some death wish, hey?" Boeta mocked as we climbed on to the Jeep.

"Well, man, any more food could have killed us. We must get a death wish again. We must do it again soon," Harry said and tamped his pipe and lit it contentedly.

On the track back to Lisala we spotted a nest in the top of a palm tree near the road. Rebel snipers built these nests in the palms by folding in fronds and using them as camouflage to fire on convoys which passed below. They were fairly easy to see if anyone looked up at the high tops of the tall palms. Many people never look skywards, and the snipers made use of that fact. In fact most people never look up at the sky at all, but this sniper's nest was occupied. The leaves used to build it gave it away as they had dried out and were a different colour and shape to the others.

"Time to see if that Tommy gun of yours is any fucking good," Boeta said to me. "That sod will only shoot at us once we are past. Stop under the tree and let's see if you can use your toy."

"Don't I get to play?" Harry asked.

The Jeep came to a stop just before the roadside palm rearing out of the tangled forest, now almost overhead. Pretending to stretch I had a good look up at the dark blob in the folded fronds of the towering palm. I pretended to look around some more, and at the same time I pushed off the safety catch. Moving fast I put the

Tommy gun up almost vertical. A long twenty-round bust of the heavy lead slugs which emptied the drum chattered loudly in the brooding stillness of the jungle. Several of the fronds drifted down from the crest of the palm tree and, as they drifted to the ground, a body launched from the nest and fell into the undergrowth, head first and obviously lifeless.

"That'll teach you, you stupid black bastard," muttered Boeta. "Good shooting Smiler."

Over the next three weeks or so the established patrol routine kept us busy. Constant ambushes were blasted away with the full firepower and the intervals between ambushes became longer. The rebels were learning at last to fear the twin-Jeep patrols. It was on one such routine patrol I killed a man, a man whose death later bothered me. Many other men had died by my hand before that man: at the first fight in the road, in ambush sites, in towns, unnumbered deaths. Those many dead men had meant nothing to me and caused me no emotion. It was rather lack of any emotion the deaths caused which worried me and my mind churned it over in the dark, sleepless dog hours of night.

That particular day when I killed a man that caused me pain, the patrol was returning after a long day, and had been ambushed four times on a new stretch of track. In those fights I had certainly killed. Nearer Lisala, to one side of the road, a substantial village of brick-built rondavels ran one side of the road, built in single file at the edge of the jungle in a cleared space. The village had been deserted each of the many times the convoy drove past. Perhaps the inhabitants heard the convoy coming and fled and hid. Matahari was, by then, loyal to Boeta and travelled in our Jeep on the patrols. It had been a long, hard, dangerous day and now home was near our vigilance decreased. No ambushes had been set this close to town for many days; armed opposition had been badly mauled along this often used part of the track. Ambushes only occurred a long way out of town where the news had not yet reached, where armed men still foolishly fired on the mercenary patrols.

"Mulele, Mulele," Matahari shouted in my ear. In the doorway of one of the huts stood a muscled, naked man. Without thought I braked to a stop, stood and shouldered the rifle. The range was no more than 30 metres. The bullet made a mark in the centre of the naked man's chest. The second round landed near the first and the man slumped to the floor, lying half outside of the hut doorway. At that death a sudden feeling of dread and unease hit. Why had I shot the man? What made me do that? Was he really a Simba? As the dead man had stood watching the two Jeeps pass he was naked. That surely meant he had been doctored, had the witch-doctor's magic water sprinkled on him, the magic water called Mulele-mia. He was a Simba rebel, the enemy and to be shot on sight.

Knowing that did not stop my feeling of guilt. Later in the quiet of the night my thoughts boiled and bubbled. There was some emotion now and that was disturbing. Yet overall there was still a feeling of indifference and it did not mean as much as it should. Had I seen too much cruelty and death? Were my emotions now beginning to demand I avoid any further killing? I reasoned with myself. If pity became the norm then misery would be my lot all day and every day. A mercenary is paid to kill. Any rationalizing to avoid that fact would not help. Today, many years later and with a lot of understanding, the death of that man at the hut door, and a few of the many who died by my hand, still bother me. Each one who bothers me is different to those shot in the heat of combat; these men were killed in exceptional circumstances. It is easy to kill in the hot-blooded heat of battle and then forget. Those I remember were not killed in the rage of battle. That man and a few others were more personal and still haunt me. They haunt me although I know nothing about them, neither their names nor anything else about them. They were complete strangers and apart from their deaths have no connection to me. Would it be easier to bear if some details about them were known?

Days passed in a haze of distorted time and no clear orders came from Wilson and the men of his chosen circle. Information on operational matters came second- and third-hand from idle talk. That was the same way word came that the Commando would soon move on. Down the scuttlebutt line passed the news of a move up the river to Bumba, the next town, about fifty kilometres away. The entire complement of transport, eight Jeeps and two seven-ton trucks, would be used. The trucks would carry ammunition and fuel, and everything else not on the Jeeps, including the extra men. This was exciting to me and most of the other men as the routine had become boring and still uppermost was the need to find loot and get rich. A new town could be Eldorado.

On the vehicle patrols out of Lisala trees often blocked the tracks. Some had been cut to slow the vehicles down for ambush, some were natural falls. If it was an ambush the Simba waited for the Jeeps to stop before firing. Normally the trees had to be cleared before it was possible to move on, as the dense jungle did not allow driving off the track. The ambush was then cleared, as usual, by a hail of bullets from our guns, and the tree cleared by chopping it up and towing it off the centre of the road. For that reason a two-metre-long, two-handed crosscut saw, ideal for cutting logs, had been taken from the mission workshop. When it was not in use the saw was tied to the front bumper of our Jeep with the long, wicked-looking teeth facing forward. The saw was the mascot of our Jeep; one of the other Jeeps had a glass bottle fixed to the grill, in which were genitals in petrol pickle, removed from a dead Simba. Another Jeep mounted a skull on the radiator. It was in fashion to have a mascot.

With increasing impatience we waited out the days before the rumoured move happened. The delay happened because the head office staff at 5 Commando Group needed to be kept in the picture. The Commando had no direct communication with headquarters at Kamina. The phones seemed to work, but there were no directories to be found and even the exchange number was unknown. There were no two-way radios. The local radio station carried some news but in Lingala or French. Virtually no information on the progress of our personal little war was to be had. No government agency still functioned in the town. The shops were empty, looted and with smashed doors and windows. We were virtually isolated from the rest. Messages were sent back and forth with the American pilots.

By this time there were two street markets in Lisala which sold a few vegetables, but the local traders would not take the newly minted Congolese paper money. Eggs, virtually the only other food on the market, could be bought with the old government's minted coins, as they were metal which could be smelted to make arrowheads and other items. Young girls, barely out of their teens, were also available for the price of one egg. Not a satisfactory substitute for food. I hoped that a move might bring better food.

We had plenty of virtually worthless local money. Within hours of 51 Commando entering Lisala one of the Jeep units found a way into a vault at a bank where the shelves were stacked with notes. For an excited moment they believed they were very rich, but the notes were all one thousand or ten thousand Congolese Franc notes in the new money. The money was nearly, but not totally, useless. It was carried away in several iron trunks and used by anyone in the Commando who found a commodity that could be bought with it. Those commodities were very few. For the rest of the contract the 51 Commando members had large denomination notes of 'funny money' in abundance. At times the larger-sized note was used as toilet paper.

One good use found for the money was in a long-running poker school which gathered in a room each night at the school building. Sometimes American military men, Marines guarding the C-130s and pilots, joined the school. The vicious bidding in the game was systematic of the craving for adrenaline. The Americans were delighted to get ten thousand francs to one dollar. The official exchange rate was then about three hundred francs to a British pound. There was no way of getting an official exchange rate and it was only on paper. It was impossible for the Americans to win as a core piece of the game of poker is bidding. The mercenaries in the game sat on boxes full of notes, now given a value in hard currency, and raised the ante endlessly when needed until the Americans folded. Poker helped with the boredom.

The men found other amusements. Chippy and Snooky, the ex-Rhodesian Army men, discovered that a leper colony near the town grew dagga to raise funds for food. Another large tin trunk was filled, this time with the pungent dope. The trunk went everywhere the two friends went. They were addicted gamblers. Each night the poker room filled with pungent blue smoke of the weed. That was an additional handicapped faced by the Marines. What memories do those Marines have of that time?

Chippy and Snooky were slight but wiry men in the typical mould of infantrymen. They were used to a hard military life and could go on and on working at physical labour long after others were worn out. Dagga had been a drug of choice since their days in the Rhodesian Light Infantry. They formed a mutual protection cell and at odd times one or two of the other men joined them, but they were streetwise enough not to need help from others when in danger. At all times they were hyped up and cheerful, and it was impossible to tell if it was the weed that produced their mood or just the way they normally were. In combat both were nerveless and almost gay; they handled firearms with practised ease. One enduring memory was of the two of them, along with three others, crowded into the front cabin of one of the heavy trucks. The windows were rolled up. The fat reefers were passing around and the entire cabin was opaque with blue smoke. Snooky later went on to high position in the casino world.

The lack of communication also meant it was never certain that the promises of our pay being paid into our accounts were true. This uncertainty went on and on right to the end of the contract. A month or two before the end it was discovered that the headquarter paymaster with Hoare's staff had received the money from the Congolese all along but had embezzled most of it. The paymaster was tasked with paying our wages into our separate accounts at home, but he had been paying it into his own account. When he was discovered, he vanished. It was not until each Commando in the field appointed a man to watch the paymaster that some money was paid to those it belonged to, that is until some of the elected guards made a pact with the new paymaster and they too vanished with all the money. Money had been the main motivation, and if the situation had been clear at an early stage most of the mercenaries would have opted out but the lack of communications kept us there.

One evening rumours began circulating that the advance on Bumba was to begin the next morning. That night the transport was fuelled from drums at the Congolese Army base. The Congolese were also coerced to hand over as much ammunition as could be found. Our transport was eight ex-USA army Jeeps and two trucks, both ten-ton Swedish Scanias. On each Jeep was mounted a forward-facing machine gun and on the roof of each truck a .30 Browning mounted to fire over the cab, the gunner standing up in the back. Of 1950s' manufacture and only recently taken out of mothballs, the Jeeps were essentially brand-new.

Most men carried rifles, the 7.62mm FN, but some preferred sub-machine guns, which were French, made and originally issued to the Belgian Army. This was the MAT 49, once a preferred weapon in the French Foreign Legion. There was also an assortment of sub-machine guns and even the drum-fed Tommy gun was still around. Nearly every man had acquired and carried a hand gun of some sort; most favoured an automatic of 9mm calibre. The handguns were nearly all collected from enemy dead. Ammunition was plentiful for the 9mm Parabellum hard nose. But there was a wide selection of other hand guns and ammunition was difficult to find; in any event the pistols were seldom if ever used in combat. Executing wounded men was their main role.

On a typical hot, misty and humid early morning the convoy headed north up river. Lisala was by then totally dysfunctional as a town and in the process of being reclaimed by the jungle. The same fate has overtaken scores of colonial towns since the advent of black rule in Africa. What the white men built has been left to rot and decay. Nothing is maintained or renewed, nothing new built. Some of it is because of hate of the white man and what he built but mostly the rot is incompetence and ignorance. The tropical jungles of Central Africa are busily making ruins for future archaeologists to find.

8

The jungle road out of Lisala had been driven over and cleared many times, and at regular intervals the moist air mixed with the stench of rotting corpses. The ugly remains of rotten bodies lay at the side of the track, bones and tattered clothing all that remained. These sites were of long-forgotten previous firefights. No-one had claimed and buried the dead. It was the rainy season and the road was deep, red mud and slippery so the corpses were pressed into the mud and partially buried when the trucks ran over them. The rainforest crowded the road menacingly and the massive trees met overhead so the route led through the familiar green tunnel. At long intervals there were villages along the road, and there the jungle had been cleared back for the odd field of banana trees. There was no sign of human life in any village. The sound of trucks coming drove the people into the safety of the forest. Sometimes a mistake had been made in the haste to leave, and a cooking fire in a thatched hut leaked blue smoke into the thick air. Even the dogs and chickens had been locked away. If a plantation was found with the short fat plantains a halt was at once called and the trees raided; the sweet, sticky, fat banana was a much sought-after food. The taste was less cloying than conventional bananas and they were much sweeter.

Once the limit of previous patrols had been reached another halt was called. Wilson and his chosen in the leading Jeep now fell back and mine and another Jeep moved to the van. The order of advance from then on was two vehicles abreast with the other Jeeps, also two abreast, following. The track was just wide enough for two. Wilson and his pals boarded one of the trucks immediately behind the column of Jeeps. He explained carefully that better control over the convoy could be kept from there. This was true, but at the time it looked to me very much like fear.

"The privilege of rank, old boy," Harry said. He was feeling tense and his pipe was clamped in his back teeth. "Nothing wrong with that."

"They're fucking shitting themselves. What the hell, it gives us first crack at the fucking Simba, hey?" Boeta said, his grey eyes sparkling in anticipation.

As the column moved on Boeta kept a thin smile on his face and his pale grey eyes watched the road intently. He hunched forward while looking hard at the road and forest ahead, his whole attitude that of a man wanting a fight. There were many swamp areas in this region, and one rose out of the dense vegetation as the column advanced. The road became a causeway. It was raised above the swamp waters much like a dam wall, but wider; it had been built to allow two trucks to pass each other without one being forced off the road into the swampy water. Each side of the causeway shallow lakes had bamboo and the odd tree growing in them. When the road widened into the causeway the two Jeeps behind moved up so there were now four abreast in the road at the van, another four Jeeps close behind and the trucks to the rear.

The surface of the causeway was smooth packed gravel and the pace of the advance increased. Two hundred metres ahead the road swept round a long right-hand curve. The curve prevented sight of what was ahead, and all that could be seen was more swamp and crowding jungle. As the column approached and then entered the curve, the sound of a deep bass chanting from many male throats rose over the hum of the engine. We in the lead slowed down and stopped, confused and unsure what to do next. Wilson brought up the truck close behind the last Jeep. He was standing in the back of the truck and height allowed him to see further down the road. He shouted in a clear voice that carried over the bass chanting; there were rebels on the road ahead.

"Charge, charge," he shouted. At the same time he waved his arm towards the road ahead. Probably he meant "attack" but he was trained as a cavalry officer and charge was the order given and carried out. Accelerating hard down the road four abreast the Jeeps, followed by the trucks, swept towards and then round the concealing bend. A great gathering of men on the road ahead came into sight. The massed men blocked the road completely from one side to the other and reached back, closely packed, along the causeway for a hundred metres or more. Perhaps a thousand men were in sight on the road and suddenly a blue cloud of gunsmoke puffed and drifted above the mass. The bass chanting increased in volume, and then the crack and hissing whiplash of bullets followed by the boom of rifles firing rattled the steamy morning.

My own rifle was in my lap, the muzzle pointing outwards. There were no doors on the Jeeps. My left hand gripped the steering wheel; my right gripped the rifle pistol grip and slipped the safety catch. The leading four Jeeps' mounted machine guns were yammering away in long angry bursts like a demented choir. Harry and Matahari, like the other men in adjoining Jeeps, were leaning far out of the back and shooting at the massed men ahead. As many guns as could be brought to bear were firing rapidly. Men standing in the back of the trucks fired over the Jeeps.

As the column hurtled up the causeway at the rebels the certainty and finality of death filled me with immense fear and rage. The distance was closing rapidly and soon the Jeep would be right among the Simba who would then be shooting from all sides at point-blank range. There is no escape from bullets fired from so close. Death was closing in at pace and when the charging Jeeps were no more than thirty metres from the nearest Simba the massed ranks broke and began to turn. Scores had fallen to the hail of bullets. Once flight and panic set in the rebels gave up any thoughts of aggression and scrambled en masse to get out of the way of the Jeeps and hail of bullets. The men in the trucks, standing high, continued to fire at the rebels over the heads of the men in the Jeeps. In front of the windscreen was a confusion of panicked and fleeing men and each second more flopped and died, the bullets slamming men down on the road and in the water like a giant's fist.

The fleeing Simba first tried to run back along the causeway but soon realized there was no escape from the bullets so scrambled headlong into the swamp. There they floundered heavily in the muddy water desperately trying to get away from the road of thunderous death. And the thunder of the Commando guns was incessant and thunderous. As the lead Jeeps arrived at the place where men had leapt off the causeway, rebels were still near the road splashing desperately through the water. The rifle fired from my lap with one hand sideways out the side of the Jeep without aim. Some of the Simba in line of fire fell and vanished underwater at the shots. The accelerator pedal was almost flat to the floor but the other drivers managed to stay alongside. The rapid charge closed with those totally panicked Simba still trying to run away down the causeway.

Boeta was firing long continual bursts, swivelling the machine gun frantically and as rapidly as he could from side to side. Unable to avoid all the fleeing Simba I ran down at least two, maybe more. Rage, anger, confusion and adrenaline were very high. Suddenly the road ahead of the Jeep was empty. I slowed, stopped and swung the Jeep round to bring the machine gun to bear on the men fleeing through the swamp and so did the other Jeeps. Mercenaries got out and stood firing repeatedly at the remaining and scattered rebels, the pitiful few who had been massed to oppose us not minutes before were now the pitiful few fleeing exhausted through the waist-deep waters. Very, very few managed to reach the shelter of long swamp grass or denser forest.

When the firing stuttered to a stop the swamp waters each side of the causeway were muddy with great patches of pinkish blood boiling up to the surface. The causeway and the slopes each side down to the water were closely littered with bodies. Leaping out to check the front of the Jeep and the radiator for damaged I noted the crosscut saw teeth had flesh and bone wedged in them. The grill of the radiator was dented by the Simba knocked down but fortunately did not have a hole. Wilson ordered the convoy to press on, so there was no time to loot the dead. The hurry to go forward also saved the wounded from being shot. The advance formed up again and went on four Jeeps abreast until, after about five kilometres, the causeway and swamp ended and the track closed down to a single lane through the jungle. Boeta leant over and punched me hard several time on the shoulder in excitement.

There were only two sorts of cigarettes to be had, Belgia Red or Belgia Blue. The Blue sort was in good supply and usually easy to get but that was because they were almost impossible to smoke. They were pungent and so rough and powerful few smokers could use them. But now one of the very strong Blues gave a comfort that was very welcome. At times when all was fear and its companion, rage, the dagga option looked very attractive. Many of the Commando were smoking it now, but there was still a built-in aversion to drugs in me. Funny that alcohol was never counted as a drug. My hands shook and my mouth was bone dry. The water in my bottle was lukewarm, but tasted sweet as honey. The smell of Harry's pipe was somehow familiar and comforting. The smell of fresh blood and bodily fluids cloyed all my senses until he puffed that aromatic smoke.

Bumba was the next town north towards the rebel capital of Stanleyville. Bumba was on the river as Lisala had been; but Lisala was in thick, tropical jungle and unless one was actually on the river bank the water was not visible. Going north the jungle thinned out a bit and there was not so much undergrowth. The road did not run through a green tunnel all the time. In places the forest was made up of very tall trees, copies of the American redwood, while sparse scrub filled open places between. The country had turned into gently rolling hills, the road running down one side of a hill and then on up the other. About an hour out of Bumba there was the inevitable road block.

Every road in Africa has a block on it. Today, as in bygone centuries, the road block is part of Africa. Fifty years ago in the Congo they were a means of enabling those with weapons to extract payment in cash or kind from road users. For many years before that tribal chiefs tolled their lands and today the inevitable roadblocks are still manned by armed men, usually by officials who extract toll in the name of the governments. Often they are manned by freebooters in countries, and there are many in Africa, where the law does not apply. That road block outside Bumba, was manned by the Mulele's Simba rebels with intent to milk road-users. It was a makeshift pole on drums blocking the road and there were grass shelters at the side of the road in which the toll keepers lurked ready to spring out like spiders in a web. The toll keepers that day at Bumba were expecting easily fleeced victims; males paid money, females supplied their bodies. They were unaware of the coming danger. The talking drums had not yet fed them the news of the events less than an hour previously.

The fast charge with guns blazing had worked so well earlier it was thereafter adopted as the best tactic. It became a favourite tactic for 51 Commando only because Wilson was from a cavalry regiment. He had ordered a charge and it, luckily, proved ideal against the poorly-trained men we were fighting. The rebel opposition understood the law of the jungle, and feared that law more than any made by man. Their law dictated that the fastest and strongest gunmen were the most feared. The unknown and frightening tactic of charging the enemy at top speed with guns blazing put us at the top of the food chain. That might was right was the only law here. The primitive tribesmen, who, for the most part, made up the rebel forces, could never steel themselves to stand and fight against Jeeps charging down the track at high speed with machine guns firing. They saw a mighty force sent by strong magic to punish them.

The same fast charge was used on the road just outside Bumba that day. The convoy first stopped hundreds of metres back while Matahari was asked for advice. His advice was that the roadblock was certainly a rebel one as Bumba had been in Simba hands for a long time. Two Jeeps led and the others followed close behind as the narrow road allowed only two vehicles abreast. Harry, now back behind our machine gun, had fed a new-two-hundred-round belt to the Browning. At less than a hundred metres out rebels, alerted by the sound of our engines, scrambled from the grass shelters and began firing guns. It was far too late and they were all smashed down long before we reached the pole which blocked the road. More of our own guns opened fire into the surrounding forest as a Jeep bumped the pole off the drums. The rush forward into town had been impeded for a few seconds. There had been no return fire from the enemy after the first hasty shots. The butterflies, following scent trails, flew in small clouds from the nearby vegetation to sip the fresh mineralized blood.

The Simba rebels used two primary methods of aiming when firing a rifle. Few of them had any idea what the sights were for. One method was to hold the rifle pointed in the direction of the enemy with both hands in front of the body and make little stabs at the enemy pulling the trigger at the same time. The other was to tuck the butt of the rifle under an armpit and line the top of the barrel with the target. Both methods resulted in most rounds whispering past us. However, when a rebel was seen to be taking a proper aim all the Commando's guns at once focused on that man. When a bullet cracked loudly in the air and hissed by signalling a near miss, the source of that shot was always got full attention. Only one man of 51 Commando was killed by rebels while in action on the first contract, the only one I observed, and that was Ian. A few men were wounded, some fairly seriously. The low casualty count can be ascribed entirely to the inability of the Simba to aim a rifle correctly.

A modern rifle spits out a bullet that at combat distance, out to about a hundred metres, goes in almost a straight line. In the conditions in the jungle that was an extreme distance of sight. After that the bullet drops considerably. In battle a near miss causes no harm. Throughout black Africa ragged armed men use modern guns with no training or familiarization. In the days of muzzle loaders that might have been adequate as the old weapons fired bullets on a trajectory much the same as an arrow, but with the advent of modern rifle this is no longer true. The one reason the AK-47 is so popular with African revolutionary forces, apart from it being available free and in large quantities from the Russians, is because it can be used to shoot much like using a water hose. The AK-47 can be pointed and fired on automatic spraying bullets widely and sometimes scoring a lucky hit. A belt-fed heavy machine gun mounted on an old truck is also a favourite as it can be used in the same way. A tremendous amount of ammunition is fired off at nothing in the incessant modern African skirmishes. It is true also those soldiers feel secure when their own guns are firing in full voice.

The road block was brushed aside and the advance rushed on into Bumba. On all sides rebels were sighted as they fled towards the forests ringing the town. Word had obviously now reached them in town that the bearded giants were closing. The stone giants with black beards and a gun in each hand were on the attack, not the Congolese Army. Harry worked hard to bring the Browning to bear on the fleeing groups. He swivelled it as far as he could to track them; at times he hung out the side of the truck. Boeta wanted to stop and chase after each group of runners and finish them all off, but the other transports were pressing from behind, and Wilson waved us on from the truck if we slowed for too long. I don't know why, probably a boyhood need to fire guns, but I wanted to try my hand with the machine gun and Harry reluctantly swapped, taking over the wheel of the Jeep. Boeta was standing braced in the back firing non-stop at distant figures. Matahari sat the other side of the truck and, although armed with an FN, just watched calmly. He, like the entire Commando, was thinking of the loot to be had in the freshly liberated town.

The tribesmen at this end of the world always seemed to get information of an event shortly after it happened. Sometimes news passed from man to distant man via shouts. That system worked just as well and rapidly where the telephone no longer worked. Then there were the talking drums. News spread by the drums faster and further than shouting. In almost every jungle village was a battery of wooden drums of different sizes and timbres; skills with the drums were passed down from father to son. Almost always, day and night, after the unit had attacked or been attacked, the tenor and bass drums would boom-tap-tap long messages with short answers coming back from deeper in the forest. They sounded like they were using some sort of complicated Morse code. The drums were chattering from the deeper jungle when the column entered Bumba. As we drove we could hear them near and far. At times when the forest was still it was possible to hear three or four different drum voices chattering and receding further and further. At night the sound of the drumming carried very far.

As the advance went on people fleeing from it were no longer only Simba rebels. The difference between ordinary locals and rebels had become clearer. Locals were not armed in any way and some were women and children. Clearly the population used to the Congolese Army, were rapidly leaving town with the fleeing Simba. The black Congolese Army soldiers had declined to join the attack from Lisala. Word had been sent to us they could not advance from Lisala before the next day as there was no petrol to fuel the transport. Firing from the moving Jeeps probably killed some locals. Many were running together with the fleeing rebels, who were armed and firing guns in the air or over their shoulders as they ran. Behind the Browning I noticed this and held back on firing at runners until sure they were Simba rebels and carrying arms. The advance headed for the airstrip. A Hercules C-130 was circling overhead and the runway had to be secured. The strip and houses of the town were visible on the flanks of the gently rolling hills. From the bottom of one hill approaching the strip I saw a long line of armed men run along the next hill. They were running through waist-high grass, possibly along a footpath so only their top half was showing.

Harry slowed to a near stop so the Browning could be swivelled to bear on the running men. The ammunition belts were loaded one in five with red tracer. Both the peep sight and the red marker bullets corrected my aim. A long burst started at the last man in line and ran through the line of running men to the front and began to track back again. During that firing all the runners fell down and vanished in the long yellow grass. I did not get a chance to visit the place later. That meant there was no way to discover if all those runners had been killed by my fire; the red tracer had marked the bullets flying true to aim. At a guess there had been about fifteen men in that line.

When I had time to think about it later my mind shied away from the actual facts. I argued with myself in the dark of night that it was unlikely they had all been killed; some of them would have heard the bullets strike others, fallen down and crawled away in the grass. Some would have been hit but only wounded. Some would have escaped. Whichever way I twisted it, it always sat heavily on me. Why? Maybe it was just too many dead at one time. Whatever it was that bothered me about that line of running men still haunts me today more than fifty years on. Yet they were just a few of the many I killed. There is no explanation I can think of as to why some affected me more than others.

After the buildings at the airstrip had been cleared the Commando drove to the end of the strip shooting up any likely ambush spots and minutes later a C-130 cargo plane with its Marine guard landed and off-loaded rations and ammunition. They also brought news that confirmed rumours which had been around for some time; firstly that the Commando would shortly be getting air support and also a massed attack on Stanleyville was planned. Some burly men in jeans and T-shirts drove a new, modern Jeep down the aircraft ramp and away towards the commercial centre. This was American intelligence at work. When the ammunition and food hit the ground there was an unruly scramble to grab as much as possible. All the empty space in the Jeep was soon crammed with ration packs. Then the four of us sat on the ground under the wing of the big plane and made an instant meal of chocolate coconut biscuits and heavily sugared coffee. For days after a resupply everyone was chewing gum. The GI packs were much better than those supplied to the Belgian Army. There were many hungry men and the food never lasted as long as the chewing gum did.

Before all hostile firing had stopped, but when there were no more running men seen on the streets, thoughts turned to looting. Boeta and Harry had heard of a Government bank in town. Apparently everyone else had heard the same as each Jeep and truck now sped off towards the commercial centre of the town. The towns in the forest next the Congo River are built, where possible, on higher ground to avoid heat and insects. Bumba was one such. We quickly found some locals cowering in a residential house. Matahari calmed them and asked where the bank was. Amazed and grateful to be alive, they directed us to it without a murmur of dissent.

Our own arrival at the bank had been very quick. The bank building was a big, ornate colonial structure with a wide flight of stairs running to wide glass and marble front walls. While we were still debating the best method of attacking the vault, the glass front wall shattered as one of 51 Commando Jeeps came though it and then bounced heavily down the front stairs. They had been faster but, as usual, even they were too late, for the vaults were empty and the building had already been looted of all valuables. For a while we searched likely looking shops but only a few reams of cloth and some cigarettes missed by previous looters could be found. Matahari loaded up the cloth on one of the trucks. Eventually he had two trucks of his own trailing along in the wake of our small convoy, heavily loaded with cloth and other tradable goods.

The mighty Congo River here at Bumba was visible from the streets of the town. A couple of days later the Congolese soldiers arrived and the inevitable wave of executions were carried out on the bank of the river and for days bloated corpses bobbed and floated on the water, trapped by water hyacinth. The scale of the Congolese Army killing was minor compared to Lisala. Intervention was carried out at once as we knew there was no danger to our own lives. Soon the Congolese soldiers got used to the idea that killing civilians was not war. Fear was the main motivation of the executions, fear that the rebels were somewhere hidden in the local population ready to counter-attack and visit revenge.

The same fear had haunted all of us during the retreat outside Lisala and later when we first entered the town, but the realization that the rebels were very weak and had no stomach for war came soon. It was then that the mercenaries stopped fearing the enemy. When the Commando stopped shooting on sight many lives were saved. The Simba rebels and the Congolese Army were much the same when it came to fear-fuelled murder. Both groups postured as crack troops, but were in mortal fear of any fighting and of each other. The men of both groups were untrained and unpaid, acting as soldiers. The orgy of murder was a reaction to fear; shooting everyone who might remotely be the enemy was a fear-filled reaction. We learnt and quickly got over our fear; the black soldiers seemed unable to get over their own.

The little riverside town must once have been a tropical paradise for the white population who lived in the neat solid houses on the hills above the river out of reach of the mosquitoes. The wide roads were lined with flowering trees and all the gardens were lushly planted with flowers and shrubs. Tall trees shaded the houses. Street lights, now broken, lined each road. There had once been nightclubs and tennis courts. They once used swimming pools and ten-pin bowling halls. But it had been three or four years since the whites fled and now decay was everywhere. Nothing had been maintained. The street lights were broken and the lines stolen; everywhere the vegetation was swallowing the town. The blacks had taken over the houses until they required maintenance and then they looted the doors and roof and windows and built huts in nearby clearings in the jungle with the spoils. The clock was everywhere turning back to pre-colonial times.

The living quarters 51 Commando took over in Bumba was an empty and grand double-storey house overlooking the river. It was fully furnished and the shower worked, although it was cold water. My own bed was on a balcony on the second floor overlooking the river. There was a bed and mattress with sheers. It made me wonder what had happened to the owner; that is if ownership of property was still possible. It was a secure and safe building that would resist all but professional soldiers attacking. There was a lockable drawer next to the bed and I made sure that my spare magazines were put there when I took them off.

Daily road-clearing patrols began again. Every morning the Jeeps drove the tracks to the north out of town shooting up ambushes. It was a repeat of Lisala. And like that town the ambushes soon became few and far between and it became rare now for the Simba to actually initiate an attack. Mostly a shot or two was fired from far up the road or forest and once or twice a grenade tossed from the undergrowth, usually falling far short. At this time firing at any likely ambush spot to pre-empt attack became another adopted tactic. It started out of boredom and just went on from there. This reconnaissance by fire was extremely hard on the ears, especially when driving a truck as I did later. The firing went on for hours, all the way out and all the way back. The more the men fired at likely hiding places the more they seemed to need to do it; it became like a drug habit.

Wilson was seen less and less by the rank and file. He and his chosen men took to staying indoors most of the time. Rumour was he had taken to smoking dagga in excess. He really was too much of a gentleman to be comfortable in the command he had taken on; that was obvious from the first day. The odd glimpses I caught of him confirmed he was a physically changed man. He looked very gaunt, unshaven and haunted. He issued no daily orders and each section of eight or so men did very much as they pleased. Apart from the ongoing battle for food the days began to drag. There was not enough excitement and the tide of adrenaline was low. This was something that kept coming up and it led to some excess.

Then the long-awaited word came to leave Bumba and fly back to Kamina in Katanga where the Commando would be joining the assault to relieve Stanleyville and rescue the white hostages there. 51 Commando would be joining up with several other Commando units. There would also be men from 6 Commando joining in the big attack. There had been no news of what other units of 5 Commando Group had been doing for the last months while we had been in the central rainforests. There had been no contact with anybody except the Americans, who knew more about the overall picture than any of the mercenaries did. But the Americans always treated information as secret and getting detailed information out of them was hard work. A normal army unit would not go into action without intelligence. We did it all the time.

The rations packs had long been depleted and hunger was again the order of the day. One morning, shortly before leaving Bumba, a group of us went out onto the big, wide river with a crate of grenades. Large fish could be seen from the banks of the river swimming just below the surface. Several dugout canoes were pressed into use. When the canoes had been manoeuvred to form a wide circle the grenades were tossed into the water. The throw was synchronized so the grenades exploded at the almost the same time. Our timing was more or less right and the grenades did explode in near unison deep down and soon large, stunned fish floated to the surface. Those fish made very welcome eating and memorable meals. They were char-grilled over an open fire. The American ration packs had become unpalatable after weeks of little else; although they were missed when they ran out. The flame-grilled fish were a sharp contrast to the pork and beans.

Suddenly one morning the Commando moved to the airstrip and we waited in the moist air as an Air Sabena plane, a four-engined DC-6, landed. The men boarded and flew back south to Katanga. It felt to me as if an entire lifetime was being left behind. As the plane gained height it was like surfacing from a deep pool, breaking out of the depths into the air to breathe again. For the first time in months, on that plane south, fear was not a constant. Fear had been all encompassing and it was not until the plane lifted into the clouds safely away from the mighty river and fetid jungle that it became apparent just how comprehensive it had been. It had been so constant that it had become daily bread and almost went unnoticed. The human can adapt to almost anything.

9

The Commando had taken on a menagerie of pets by the time they withdrew from Bumba, and those pets were also going south. There were some small Capuchin monkeys, with red and round faces fringed with white hair and a number of African grey as well as other parrots. It seems to be in the nature of man to collect animals to make pets whenever they can. There was no chance of these pets ever being allowed across the border into South Africa and yet the collection grew, and later on nearly every mercenary had a pet. The monkeys adapted quickly to any room in which they were put as long as they had food and water. The apes could easily be left alone in the room for a day while the owners were away. The parrots had been trained by the hunters who had captured them to come at a whistle, each bird had its own. The parrots usually stayed in nearby trees during the day when the new owners were away and came to the whistler when called. The local tribesmen showed us if a bird was fed on a pawpaw it would come to sit on the owners arm when called. Apparently pawpaw seeds were much sought-after by the birds. The magic pawpaw worked as a sort of invisible leash keeping the birds nearby.

That Air Sabena DC-6 passenger plane taking us south was fitted as a civilian plane and the Commando was in relative luxury in the plush seats and air conditioning. It was mid-summer over tropical Africa. One moment the plane was droning along and the next a massive turbulence of a gathering tropical storm hit. The plane fell over a thousand metres in a massive air pocket and was tossed about so that it was flying wing down and then wing up, the nose rising and falling, and more air pockets produced sudden falls that ended with a sickening thump. The monkeys and parrots did not have anything to hold on to and the air above the seats was dotted with airborne pets each time the plane hit an air pocket. The massive turbulence ended as suddenly as it had started; a very worried co-pilot came down the aisle and inspected each wing through the windows. It was later learnt that the wings had cracked where they joined the fuselage. That plane never flew again but was left to rot at the Kamina airport.

There was plenty of time to sit and think on that flight and once the frightening turbulence was over my mind went back over the last months. I still could not decide how many men I had killed. This enormous question occupied a lot of my quiet time. Certainly there had been many in the heat of battle and while they were, if only feebly, trying to kill me. I was unable to count them in my mind, even by concentrating and thinking carefully. There had been so many ambushes and quick firefights in the jungle I had lost count of those as well; it all melded together in one time and space. Many times the enemy had been killed without even being in sight. The Simba, except for the pitched battles on the roads to town, always hid away in the undergrowth. The vegetation did not provide cover from bullets and many of them died there unseen. At the major battles on the road my rifle had been fired until it was too hot to hold, and the men I aimed at went down, but with all the other mercenaries firing at the same time it was hard to tell for certain if the rebel who fell was not cut down by another's bullet. That long line of running men who fell under the tracer fire? Don't think of that.

While pondering on my score my mind dragged up an incident I had tried hard to forget, and yet it had often taken me by surprise before I could blank it off. Boeta and I were alone in the Jeep out buying eggs. The native village was on the outskirts of Bumba and the women were called to from the Jeep to bring eggs. Old regime coins were used, and at each stop we garnered one or two eggs. It was a warm day and a light breeze was blowing, which makes for ease and relaxation. Then a sniper shot cracked the stillness open from a cluster of houses to the right of the road. We both stood up in the Jeep and searched the houses with our rifles up and ready. It was fairly easy to tell which house the shots were coming from. The shooter's bullets did not come close; they cracked far overhead without the whistle of a near miss.

The sniper had to be killed, the fighting rage boiled hot, and we began to walk towards the house, rifles at the port hoping for a glimpse of the sniper. When fifty metres from the house, a young man dressed in tattered shorts and shirt ran out the door and galloped away. Boeta shouted for him to "come here" in Lingala; "Oye awa" but he did not stop and my FN lifted and fired in a reflex action. A running target needs to be led and I had plenty of practice on running buck. The man was frantically running past a cattle kraal of thin, hard upright poles and the bullet went through a pole before hitting him in the mid-section. The bullet had expanded and splintered and cut the man in half, the top half of his torso fell backwards, his stomach organs came out, his legs remained upright so he was folded in half backwards, his head by his bare feet. Butterflies began to gather and the cloying smell of fresh blood mingled with that of body fluids from the stomach, the smell of a slaughtered cow. The butterflies flitted out of nowhere and the blue flies buzzed, all in seconds.

The sight was horrifying and grizzly, but Boeta grinned widely and gave the thumbs up. "Fucking good shot, Smiler. Teach the little shit to shoot at us. Fuck that bullet must have mushroomed, look at that. Never seen anything like. Wish we had a camera."

During those days that stretched back like a lifetime since Kamina, many men had died by my hand and many others had been executed in my sight. The screams of those being tortured and raped by the black troops had filled days and nights. Yet that man was one of those who stuck in my mind although I made an effort to blank it out. Those shot in the heat of a firefight left no mental scar. That man who was so badly mauled by a freak shot behind the cattle pen, and the naked one in the door of the hut outside Lisala were vividly remembered. They both haunted me, those two and some others as well. At the time of the kill there was little emotion; maybe there was too much to fear and there was no room for any other emotion. Only years later did all the killing begin to prick me. Killing is not a slight, nothing thing to do; human instinct eventually punishes those who do so and think they don't care.

By the time the plane landed at Kamina my mind had blanked it out and I fell into a doze. It was a massive relief to be out of the rainforest and tangled jungle. Here in Katanga the country was open with scattered trees and grasslands. Soon after landing the Commando straggled back to the old semi-ruined army barracks. It almost felt like returning home for some reason. At the barracks we found there were many new recruits waiting to be sent north. The recruits looked 51 Commando over warily and in silent awe. The Commando were hardened veterans to them and the newspaper-manufactured fame preceded it. We were dirty and armed, and must have looked very dangerous, which in fact we were.

The room I found for myself in the derelict building had a fairly good bed. At least all the springs were there and the dirty rubber mattress covers were only slightly torn. The plumbing had been fixed since we went away and the showers were working, albeit only cold water, and the seat-less toilets flushed. A mess room had opened and food was available. Food which was not of the ration pack variety had to be paid for as the cooks were running the kitchen as a private enterprise. The cooks had not been to the interior, however, and were not experienced in the ways of the Congo yet, so were quiet happy to accept ten thousand Congolese franc notes, of which the 51 Commando still had trunks full. There was also the usual semi-permanent Crown and Anchor game on the go in another room, and the large, ornate notes gladly accepted there as well. In normal times the place would be barely liveable but the relief of getting away from the dark heart of Africa made it feel luxurious. It felt strange not have to listen to constant screams and the thump of guns firing in the distance. It took several days to relax to a reasonable level. Even then it felt unsafe to walk anywhere without a rifle slung.

Hoare and his senior staff were at the Kamina barracks. A day came when a parade in front of the buildings was ordered and everyone fell in in ranks of three. Hoare came out to address the assembled men. There was a swagger stick gripped under his arm and he was neatly dressed in camouflage uniform and polished black boots. On his head was a beret correctly cocked over the forehead, and on the front of the beret were two brass badges. I did not recognize what unit the badges were from. Something nudged my memory to recall photographs of Field Marshal Montgomery during his Desert campaign. The two men looked a lot alike, both small in stature with bony, hooked noses. The twin badges were worn on the beret in an identical fashion. Hoare was trying deliberately to emulate Montgomery; that was my sudden thought.

There was a strong aura of command about him, a certain strength that was apparent even from a distance by the arrogant way he carried himself. When Hoare talked everyone listened. But listening to him that day gave the impression his address was mostly an act, a carefully rehearsed and studied act. He had cultivated the air of an officer in command and carried it off well, but to me it was all an act. The more I thought it was a performance the more apparent it became to me that it was so. My first feelings of that day later turned out to correct. When it came to combat, he, like so many other senior army officers everywhere, fell far short of the image they cultivated. The invincible warrior air fell away when the bullets began to sing their stuttering song. In that, of course, he was no different from all the men in the 5 Commando Group, but at least the majority of them did not try to appear fearless.

The few times I saw Hoare was when he had gathered the men together to give a speech. He was invisible at other times. Not once during the contract did I hear him give a direct order, and certainly never heard Wilson or those who replaced him relay any orders from him. We went into combat without orders from anyone senior, and the entire war, of several years, seems to have been fought without any tactical oversight. After a pep speech Hoare gave us information.

Our Commando along with one other had been in the field for some months and had been specifically recalled in order to join the combined push on Stanleyville. 51 Commando were considered by the headquarters to be experienced hard core after only less than three months of combat. Two newly formed 5 Commando Group Commandos would join in the big push as would the entire 6 Commando Group under 'Black Jack' Schramme. 6 Commando Group were men recruited mainly in Europe and many of them were Belgians. New transport was to be issued to all units and armoured vehicles would be at the van of the convoy. For a few days while the convoy was built 51 Commando idled in the tatty barracks, and as it usually does idleness brought irritation.

Congo Jack was a round-faced, jug-eared man who claimed to have fought in the previous campaign against the UN. His voice was penetrating and insistent and at every chance he got he told everyone what a veteran and hero he was. Bouncer was a tall, bony, marshmallow white and pink Cockney and a bully, as are most men who were big for their age at school. Large boys find the smaller boys are scared by their body size and get in the habit of pushing others around using that body size as a threat. The two of them had been at Kamina when we first arrived in the country and were still there after months. Both had landed cushy, dubious headquarter jobs and so never left base. They naturally attracted each other, though every army has the same sort of men.

One morning some of the precious stack of spare rifle magazines vanished from the table in my room. Congo Jack and Bouncer both habitually wore strong aftershave and antiperspirant. The scent, which my hunter's nose at once picked up, lingering in the room pointed to them as the culprits. Everyone, especially those who had been in the fighting, set a very high value on spare magazines. The cache in my room had taken time to gather. Later in the mess, in a blind rage, my suspicions were vented to all who would listen. There were still ten or so spare magazines in my webbing, more than enough, so the theft was not crucial, but the affrontery of it rankled deeply. Men had been killed for less heinous crimes than stealing spare magazines. If I had found the offenders then there would have been violence; I was itching to punch them down. The strength of my rage took me by surprise; normally I would not have been so vocal or reckless in accusations. Clearly the previous months of violence were still affecting me.

That afternoon found me lying on the tattered bed trying to cool down out of the humid heat beating down from the equatorial sun outside. Congo Jack and Bouncer burst through the door. Both carried automatic pistols, hands hanging at their sides and almost behind their backs, to partially conceal the weapons. My own rifle was against the wall and out of reach. The Colt .357 Magnum was in a drawer of a battered table in its webbing holster. The experience gained in the copper mine bars kept me very calm and unworried and so I made sure I put on an unconcerned front. Once a man shows fear in a fight, his opponent has the advantage.

"Whotcha saying, mate? That I stole from yous? Yous looking for troubles?" Bouncer demanded.

"We veterans have ways of dealing with those who cause us trouble," said Congo Jack shrilly.

"Well hello, nice of you to show up," I said, sitting up and measuring the distance to the weapons and to each man. It would be best to attack them physically and fast. The weapons were too far away. If I fumbled the weapons they might get off a few shots before me. Punching hard and fast was the way to go, first, fast and hard. Why was my pistol not on my belt? Stupid, stupid.

"Got any ting ta say, mate? Wots up, cat got yer tongue?" Bouncer queried, enjoying his obvious advantage.

"Was you guys, I would fuck off while you still can," I said, as quietly and calmly as I could.

"Ha, fucking, ha."

"Who do you think you are talking to, do you know who I am?" shrilled Congo Jack.

So the stupid violence had caught up with me here at the barracks where there had been little violence. The danger that plagued the mercenary life, being shot by fellow soldiers, had walked in through an open door unexpectedly. Well, I swore to myself, they were going to find it very hard to take me down, and my muscles tensed ready to jump them and begin punching.

A movement showed at the periphery of my vision and Boeta came silently through the open door behind Bouncer. The rifle in his hands lifted and the butt smashed Bouncer between the shoulders propelling him stumbling painfully across the room. Bouncer stuck out a hand to stop himself hitting hard against the wall, snot and tears on his face. Bouncer's pistol clattered loudly on the floor. Congo Jack gave a frightened little squeak and began to back away. There was a metallic knocking on the door frame and Harry looked round the jamb. His pipe was clenched in his back teeth, slow eyes narrowed. His rifle barrel had made the knocking.

"Hey man, do you mind if I pay a visit unannounced?" Harry drawled.

"Kill the fuckers," Boeta grated, cold eyes holding Bouncer pinned against the wall with fear.

"Sorry, sorry," Congo Jack squeaked. "Wait, wait, hold on, I'll go get the magazines. Wait, please."

"Go quickly, you got ten seconds."

A few seconds later Congo Jack ran back into the room and offered the stolen magazines to me. Bouncer was still frozen against the wall, not even daring to wipe the fluids from his white, shocked and pained face. The butt between the shoulders had been hard enough to break bones. Word of the incident was spread quickly by the men watching from the corridor, and it gave the three of us immunity at Kamina from the plague of stupidity which had killed men in other places. After the scare Bouncer and Congo Jack got that day, they left others' goods alone. They had had a profitable sideline, stealing and reselling goods for which there was a demand. The two of them were lucky to live through that event. If I had not restrained Boeta that afternoon they would have been dead on the floor of my room. The pair of them managed to draw out their stay at Kamina barracks for many more months before leaving the Congo. No doubt they boasted to the gullible about the hell of the Congo.

ↁ

A large number of white people had been taken hostage by the Simba in the Stanleyville and a rescue plan needed a fast advance over long distance if they were to be saved from execution. The little commanding officer treated the campaign he was orchestrating as if it was the invasion of Europe. 51 Commando had their own opinion; a massive column and firepower was not necessary. Experience had shown

51 Commando that this was true but it would have been hard to convince anyone who had not been there with us that a headlong reckless charge by a few fast vehicles was needed. Wilson, who had been very much the nominal head of 51 Commando for weeks, disappeared. So he was not the one to discuss it with Hoare. His English gentleman's sensibilities had taken a battering and he had opted out. His replacement was one Forbes, a tall dark man with oiled, slicked-back hair, who spoke with a pseudo-American accent but farmed maize in South Africa. Forbes, after the Congo, was rumoured to have gone to America to marry a very rich woman he met through a dating service.

It really did not matter who had nominal command of the unit. The men were used to doing as they pleased. The men on a vehicle decided what was to be done by that particular vehicle. This came about because there were seldom any orders given, and those men with pips and stripes on their shirts stayed out of the fighting and away from the front line, whenever they could. What was urgently required from the new commanding officer of 51 Commando was information of the status of our pay. Some men had letters from home delivered to the Kamina barracks and no one had seen any pay. A committee was eventually sent to Hoare which came back with more promises. In the end each Commando sent more men to the pay office to watch over the paymaster. The missing pay had all been stolen, as usual, by replacement paymasters but also by the men sent to watch that it did not happen. Hoare and the senior men had been paid, the thieves made sure of that, so they justly claimed be unaware of what was going on. The promise made to the committee was closer supervision and all backpay soon. Now more men were put in the pay office watching the men watching the paymaster.

Brand-new Ford 250 trucks with 7 ton open backs were issued. Delivery had been made by the Americans via Hercules C-130 aircraft. One of the brand new Fords became my drive. It was at once stocked with all the ammunition and food that could be scrounged or stolen. Sandbags were tied down on the roof of the cab and a newly acquired .50 Browning belt-fed machine gun mounted. As normal with our belt-fed guns, a box that swivelled with the gun was rigged so a second man was not needed to feed the belt into the gun when it was fired. The .50 was a heavy machine gun and very powerful; little could hide an enemy from its bullets.

The convoy formed up slowly over some days. By the time it was complete and ready for the road it stretched two kilometres or more. Ferret scout cars, six of them in the van, were followed by Belgian-made armoured troop carriers nicknamed 'bathtubs". Then came 5 Commando Group units; with their newly issued transport, including some newly delivered armoured Land Rovers. These vehicles were Italian Army design and had an armour-plated front and back and armoured glass screens, one in front of the driver. There was also a similar MAG on a pintle at the back for defence against aircraft. A lever near the driver closed louvers of steel in front of the radiator when needed. The entire floor had compartments in which boxes of machine-gun ammunition in two-hundred-round belts fitted. Four men manned each Land Rover and all of them carried automatic rifles and pistols. One vehicle in action could deliver the firepower of an entire Second World War infantry company, probably more. 51 Commando was issued four new Land Rovers and two of the new Ford 250 trucks. The Americans were spending big money but their objective remained secret. Maybe the American public was in the dark but certainly not the Congolese.

The two machine guns mounted pointing forward through the armoured glass had a swivelling mount. Cross hairs to aim with were etched on the swivelling glass screen. The guns came with shoulder butts that were removable and could be replaced with pistol grips. The preferred way to fire them was with the pistol grips fitted. With them in place the target was centred in cross hairs and one gun triggered. The recoil turned the guns on the centre mount sweeping towards the side of the fired gun, and then the other gun was fired and the sight swept back with the recoil across the target again. Firing alternate guns with the pistols grips in place had the guns sweep back and forth across the targets. Spray and pray: modern warfare.

All the different mercenary units began to fall in line, with 5 Commando Group's Jeeps leading the trucks that came at the rear after the armour and Jeeps. The only other Commando on the convoy beside our own to have seen any fighting was 53 Commando. It was hard to say how many other 5 Commando Group men there were on that convoy, but at a guess a hundred or so. There was also the Belgian 6 Commando Group under Schramme, who added perhaps another hundred men. 6 Commando Group were mostly in the armoured vanguard where some of them led the convoy in Ferret Scout cars and others drove the armoured personnel carriers, the 'bathtubs', which mounted a turreted machine gun up front. There were maybe over one hundred vehicles, but no one counted them and that is my guess.

There was a smattering of black troops, not as a separate unit but attached to one or other of the mercenary units. As usual no definite orders or instructions were given to us. One morning the men moved out of the barracks and boarded the transport and the front of the convoy began to move slowly down the road. 51 Commando was about half way down from the front, maybe a kilometre behind the leading armoured cars. When the convoy began to move the truck ahead of mine moved, giving the only signal for our truck to go. When the truck ahead stopped we did likewise. That went on day and night without end, in a blur of distorted time with only too-brief stops to eat and sleep. Time lost meaning after the first two days, hours blending into days. It was all long, long hours of driving with only the rear of the truck ahead in sight.

The convoy went north towards the Lualaba River, and the town of Kindu. From there it would follow the Lualaba north towards the Congo River, of which it was as tributary. The route was to be along that river, then across and on towards Stanleyville through the dense, tropical rainforests. Boeta and Harry gleaned this information by visiting other vehicles when the convoy stopped. Our small unit of mutual protection formed at Lisala remained intact. Our previous experience ensured the truck had been fully stocked with ration packs and ammunition. There were fuel tankers in the convoy but we also carried as may extra jerrycans of fuel as we could find place for.

The officers and NCOs had given no battle orders. So the main campaign of the contract started without any orders from those in charge and Stanleyville, the main objective at that time was many days' drive away, a lot of which was through rebel-held territory. Harry took over the front seat next to me in the cab. He had looted a large stock of Dutch pipe tobacco so soon the entire cab reeked of rum and herbs. Boeta had chosen to man the .50 Browning on the roof because he believed there would be more action from there. On the second day, when this proved not to be the case, he went off on his own to join a vehicle nearer the front, impatient as always for action. Three others of the Commando rode in the back, which we had covered in canvas. Whenever a short rest break happened Boeta came back to brew tea with us and give us news of any action up front a kilometre ahead.

The convoy drove for 18 to 20 hours at a stretch, with a few shorts stops for food and stopped for the night long after midnight. By first light we had moved on. Progress was very slow and cumbersome with so many vehicles. After two nights, and with almost no sleep, the number of days and nights on the road blurred into one unending journey. Driving became instinctive, follow the truck ahead; that was all that mattered. Once out of the Katanga savannah the familiar rainforests lined the road and ran through the well-known green tunnel. The damp heat of the nearby equator filled the cab. All that was visible was the truck ahead and the green walls each side. When night fell it was still only the red tail lights of the truck ahead that were visible in the blackness.

At times there were rebel ambushes on that long, long road and the Simba must have been delighted with the massed target. At irregular intervals the distant sound of gunfire came back to us from the van, the sound of heavy machine gun fire and grenades exploding. When the distant firing began the truck ahead would stop and the men would jump out and stretch. The visible road would be filled with men urinating. Then, when after a short delay the firing stopped, the convoy moved again. On and on it went, day after day and night after night, with only three or four hours to sleep.

In the dark hours of one night when all sense of time and place had been blurred, a fairly large settlement showed each side of the road in the headlights. Someone at the roadside waved, directing us to pull into an open yard where there was a large white building marked with a red cross on the white wall. Killing the truck engine and headlights, I at once fell into an exhausted asleep on the front seat, slumped against the door. Where we had stopped did not matter; only sleep was of any importance.

Something woke me a few hours later to find there was a vehicle facing ours with headlights full on. Still stunned from lack of sleep and intending to tell the driver to kill his lights as they were keeping me awake I got out of my nest. Only then, outside and on the ground, did I become aware of gunfire and shouting all around me. With pistol in hand I yanked open the offending truck's door to switch off the lights; it had now become dangerous to be lit up. As the door opened a body fell out almost on top of me. It was the driver and bullet holes in the windscreen slowly came into focus. Slowly shaking off the sleep drug with an effort I became more aware of what was going on. By then the shooting had died to sporadic shots in the dark. The machine gunner on my truck shouted down to me standing stupidly with pistol in hand, looking confusedly around, that the offending truck was a rebel one attempting to bring wounded Simba to the clinic. We were parked in the clinic grounds.

The rebels being transported to the clinic had been wounded by fire from the convoy earlier in the day at one of the road blocks when they idiotically fired on the massed armoured cars in the van instead of picking on the soft skinned vehicles further back. It had been the .50 machine gun firing from the cab roof which woke me, although it had not fully penetrated my befuddled mind. I was so stunned by lack of sleep that the loud sound a short way over my head did not register. It was all over now and fumbling off the lights in the rebel truck; I once again got back in the cab and fell asleep immediately. Sleep mattered more than anything else. What happened outside the cab was of not my concern. Sleep was impossible to deny, and all that mattered. Let someone else deal with other things outside there in the dark.

The next afternoon the convoy reached the fairly large riverside town of Kindu. There we would wait for two days for another Commando to join the convoy. That other Commando unit from 5 Commando Group had been fighting in the Kindu region for some months by then. I think they were unhappy that they had not been allowed to take Kindu as they had been fighting towards it. We had no contact with them from the town. The Lualaba River at Kindu was about two hundred metres wide and slow flowing. When the armoured head of our convoy swept into town we were expected, but not just then and the rebels were only just beginning to leave; several hundred were fleeing on a lumbering ferry crossing the river. The talking drums had been too slow with the news. The ferry was not yet a hundred metres off shore.

The armour raged along the road on the riverbank very soon after the ferry had left shore. The carnage was indescribably terrible as multiple machines guns swept the open steel decks of the barge in a deadly, sustained chattering roar. The riverbank road was straight and high and most of the guns of the convoy could be turned on the ferry. My head turned away of its own violation; I could not watch the slaughter, but the acrid smell of fountains of blood rose above the clean smell of the water. The smell was as bad as the sight. Corpses floated in the river for several days. The bodies quickly bloated like grotesque balloons, their trousers and shirts split by swollen flesh, and arms curved stiffly. The currant was slow at this wide stretch, hardly moving and the edges were lined with hyacinth.

Most of the time waiting was passed with sleep. Some men, bored with the delay, took to shooting the bloated corpses which released the gas and sank them. Wide beds of floating weeds trapped the dead. The convoy water wagon went far upstream to refill. The town had been looted by several waves, but late one afternoon our small unit went on the prowl. Odds and ends of tinned food were found, mostly abandoned by the Simba and were added to the stock in the truck. The morning sun came bright and clear with the stench of rotting bodies spoiling it. The awaited Commando had arrived in the night and the convoy again moved northwards towards the major target, Stanleyville.

It rained one night just as the convoy stopped for a brief food break. One of the truck drivers, some distance ahead, struggled to light a wood cooking fire. As all the wood was wet he siphoned petrol from the truck. The container he used was leaking and left a trail of petrol from the truck tank to the intended fire. Petrol went on the wood and a match was struck, the spilt petrol ignited the truck tank. The transport each side of the blazing truck could only move when those in front or behind them had done so. It was some time before the convoy reversed and went forward enough for the closest to move. By the time those jammed vehicles managed to get on the move it was too late for some; three other trucks caught alight and burnt out totally. Once ammunition stopped exploding the wrecks were pushed off the road. The men from them joined other trucks. It was accepted as a normal event.

In the dark of another night, in that endless drive, the convoy stopped and word came down a regular Belgian Army General had joined up with Hoare and his staff. The information was Belgian Army detachments from Europe, some of them paratroopers, had been deployed to attack Stanleyville. The reason given was that the mercenaries were not up to the task of freeing the white hostages and airborne troops would do a better job. It was still before midnight and the convoy could have been in town and scattering the rebels before dawn. There in the jungle in the endless night a conference was held by the unknown senior staff. Word then passed down that the convoy would not move for twenty-four hours. The European paratroopers would strike at dawn and were to handle the hostage matter. My doubts of Hoare deepened.

The disappointment also influenced my judgement of him. Stanleyville still had functional businesses in it and a lot of loot was to be had. That was the scuttlebutt anyway and it turned out to be wrong; little was still working. The idea of the Belgium Army having first crack did not go down well. It did not occur to any mercenary the Belgian Army would not loot. The mood that night was such that if it had been physically possible 51 Commando would have gone off alone and done the cavalry charge. It was not physically possible as we were stuck in the middle of scores of trucks in the rainforest tunnel. There was nothing left to do except sleep and wait. It was that delay, ordered by Hoare and the Belgian officer, which was directly responsible for the death of many hostages. They did not have the experience of the conditions on the ground, as we had. They were trained in conventional warfare.

The following morning word came that the Belgian paratroopers were in the city and then suddenly the convoy began to move. The outskirts of Stanleyville were reached in less than three hours. The paratroopers had dropped at the commercial airport, a good ten kilometres out of the centre of the city and had mounted a classic street-fighting offensive, with small troop carriers and heavy machine guns to back them. That unavoidable delay, the wrong tactic, had also cost the hostages lives. As the convoy drove by at speed, sections of the paratroopers in fox holes at the side of the road waved, indicating and shouting that there were enemy ahead. They were visibly amazed when the mercenaries just waved back and drove on. As they had not been opposed during the advance, the paratroopers had no way of judging the Simba inability to conduct modern warfare or street fighting. They had to assume opposition in house-to-house fighting would be stiff. The speed of the convoy entering the city that morning was as a result of greed overcoming fear. But it was the right tactic, as we would have told anyone who asked.

The massive convoy ended up in a central square in the main commercial district of the town. Hoare then issued direct orders for the first time that I was aware of. Everyone was ordered to parade in the town square and eventually formed up in their units. Sporadic gunfire could be heard from all around but it was not in the close vicinity of the paraded men. Hoare looked haggard and worn, as we all did, but his modulated voice still had the authority that marked him. He gave a stirring speech about superb fighting units and how proud he was of all. He went on to order there was to be no looting. When we formed up there were many men and vehicles of 5 Commando Group absent. They had peeled off down side roads. As Hoare ordered that there was to be no looting there came the crash of glass windows breaking and a dull explosion from a nearby bank. He pretended not to hear, ignored it and went on talking.

The delay caused by the paratroopers' conventional tactics had given the Simba rebels plenty of time. They had time to line up the hostages in the street outside the hotel where they had been kept under guard. When the sounds of fighting came closer to the hotel, the Simba had turned their guns on the hostages and then run away in panic. Another score of whites were dead and many wounded. The survivors were located by the paratroopers no more than an hour after the massacre; much, much too late for the dead. The terrified survivors were rushed under guard to the airport for evacuation. By then the mercenaries were in control of the city. It took days for the Belgian Army to accept this; it was beyond their training.

We did not visit the hostage killing ground until sometime later and then nothing was to be seen but blood stains and oddments of abandoned shoes. As there were blood stains on pavements all over the city it was not an unusual sight. 5 Commando Group later made the Hotel Stanleyville, where the massacre had taken place, their mess. Excellent meals were eaten there until the kitchen ran out of supplies. The bar was drunk dry very soon, yet we always managed to find more stocks of beer. Hoare and his head quarter officers moved in for the duration of the stay in Stanleyville. The hotel was a fine old colonial building with a tin roof and a wide wraparound veranda.

Belgian para-commandos en route to Ascension Island. (Wikicommons)

A C-130 roars in low over Stanleyville before returning to Leopoldville. (Wikicommons)

Dragon Rouge. The advance to Stanleyville. (Wikicommons)

An AS-21 tricycle moves troops into place around Stanleyville airport. (Wikicommons)

Dragon Rouge after the jump at the Stanleyville airfield. Rebels who formerly controlled the tower are stretched out on the ground as prisoners. (Wikicommons)

Major Mine and Lieutenant Legrelle confer, Stanleyville airfield. (Wikicommons)

First evacuees from the massacre at Stanleyville, 24 November. (Wikicommons)

Defending the airfield at Stanleyville. (Wikicommons)

Before the takeoff to Kamina from Paulis. (Wikicommons)

Medical evacuation. Wounded hostages receive medical aid. (Wikicommons)

Para-commandos at the airfield, Paulis. (Wikicommons)

Refugees on the road to the airfield. (Wikicommons)

Congo refugees. (Rhodesian Air Force)

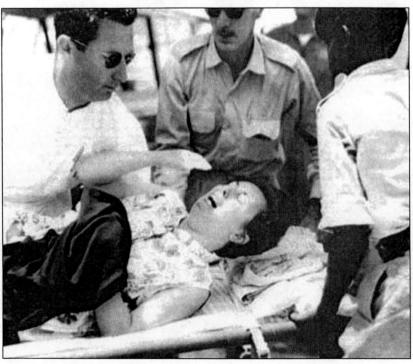

A Belgian woman in hysterics as she is transported to a departing C-130. (Wikicommons)

Dragon operations. A C-130 Hercules landing at Paulis airstrip to remove hostages and withdrawing paratroops. (Wikicommons)

Withdrawal of para-commandos to the airfield, Paulis. (Wikicommons)

This Air Congo Dakota was hijacked by members of No 6 Commando
and flown out of the Congo to Rhodesia. (Wikicommons)

President Mobutu of Zaire in his
Pentagon office. (Wikicommons)

Wearing French uniforms, berets and insignia along with Commando shoulder slides, these men may possibly be former Colonial paratroopers. (Wikicommons)

Swedish soldiers in the Congo. (Wikicommons)

10

51 Commando took over an apartment tower block on the bank of the river. They were luxury apartments and my own was split-level and had four bedrooms and three bathrooms. Each of us had a similar apartment. After doing a bit of snooping about, I discovered the place belonged to the Swedish Ambassador, who, some days later, knocked and asked for his flat back so I moved next door. The second apartment had original oil paintings on the walls and thick pile carpeting. The greatest miracle was that the electricity was still working and so the stove and other appliances could be used. The grocery cupboard was empty as were all the kitchen shelves but I broke open a locked cupboard built into the wall and found it stocked with what was probably an emergency supply of food for the previous patrons. There were platoon-size cartons of American army ration packs, each carton one meal for fifteen men. There was also a cache of many bags of Kenyan coffee and sugar, for which I would have traded magazines if offered in barter.

I kept my secret from the others as I stuffed myself with pork and beans. The cache lasted the duration of my stay in Stanleyville. Boeta and Harry noticed my rucksack bulging with food but as they made no comment, they had probably struck it lucky themselves. When I was sure they had I offered to share and, as anticipated, they declined. The beleaguered Stanleyville whites had somehow managed to collect and horde food while the city was in Simba hands. The caches were mostly American GI rations. Some of which, especially the tinned whole chicken, was almost inedible. When the can opened the whole fowl came out in one piece and had the consistency of hard set jelly. Any food was a great luxury; many of the local population only ate what the ever-present jungle and the river provided. River boats brought the only supplies to the city and they had stopped arriving many months before.

Any small unit of friends took any Jeep or truck they could find to do very much what they wanted to do in Stanleyville, because, as usual, there were no orders issued. 51 Commando boss, Forbes, was even less effective in communicating with the Commando than Wilson had been. It was hard to believe that he even existed. Each day three of us went out in the new Ford with Boeta manning the Browning on the roof and Harry scenting the cabin with his pipe. Each day we roamed the streets of the city and suburbs in search of loot. An expensive watch was found in the back of a drawer in the looted UN office. Plenty of clothing and shoes and other such stuff were found in many wrecked stores, but what we needed was valuable and less bulky loot. Matahari, then still with us but working independently, accumulated truckloads of the soft merchandise and not long afterwards sent a convoy south to his home. There he later became a rich and respected elder of his tribe. The good looting possibilities were soon exhausted as there were many mercenaries and Congolese soldiers on the prowl. When the wave of would-be looting had passed some commercial concerns and a Government bank reopened.

In many of the deserted urban homes in this part of the Congo there were carved ivory tusks. At first these were carried off by mercenaries, but in the end they proved too bulky and clumsy to cart around, especially when in action. The carved tusks could not easily be converted to money either. There was no one around who would pay US dollars for the ivory as there was enough of it going free. There was also no easy or obvious way to ship it back to South Africa or Europe. Strict laws against trade in animal parts were in force in all Western countries. A fortune in carved ivory was there for the taking, but could not be made use of. A small ivory palm tree with removable leaves ended up in my toilet bag and eventually went through customs in the unopened bag: that was the only memento taken home by me.

Near the bank of the Congo, at the edge of the city centre, there was a crumbling sports ground with a broken clubhouse and swimming pool. The water in the pool was fresh as it was pumped up from the river. The river here was about three hundred metres wide and flowing strongly so that ripples and whirls could to be seen out in the current. The pool was welcome in the hot, humid, tropical weather and used by the white mercenaries to cool down. It had become a favourite spot for the European members of 6 Commando Group who suffered most in the heat. Some of them had arrived with the main convoy and others had since come up. 6 Commando Group travelled around the city in armoured cars, usually in the 'bathtubs' or Ferret scout cars. They had another armoured car of a make unknown to me, which had a cannon and machines guns like a small tank.

The European contingent had a taste for young black girls. This taste was very obvious when we were at the pool cooling off and 6 Commando Group men were also there. Nearly all of them had two or more black teenage girls hanging on. The pubescent girls did not have proper bathing suits and dressed only in nylon panties which became transparent when wet. All around on the grass surrounding the pool there was constant casual fornication taking place. No privacy was sought or required; this was a commercial transaction not intimate sex. While rifles cracked far away and bullets swished through the air, pale backsides pumped and black legs straddled on the green grass. Nothing could distract the participants. There were far-off, small pockets of rebels in parts of the city who kept up a sporadic, aimless fire mostly from very distant high-rise buildings.

My Afrikaans upbringing quelled any desire to buy a girl, but it was not only my innate reluctance to jump the colour bar. The young girls could be bought for a few thousand francs. Government money was acceptable in the big city for goods not imported and local service, like that given by the girls. The girls were barely out of their teens, and not very experienced. My experience in Europe had left me with a taste for passionate and refined woman. The young and innocent had little appeal sexually. Quick fornication with a passive girl seemed to be no better than masturbation. My taste for experienced and expert woman left me with a disinterest in the youngsters. There was little sexual desire. Quick sex could be had in all the urban areas but left me uninterested or so I thought. There was also the threat of disease as almost no rubbers were available. In the smaller towns young women could be bought for the price of one hen's egg. Multiple partners for the young girls were the norm when the military were in town. The ease with which the Europeans and some South African whites mingled with the black women was distasteful to me. Certainly sexual disease was spread by these encounters.

My sex drive was always very strong, and just because I was not interested did not mean it had diminished; any man who is young and healthy and in mortal danger has undeniable urges to breed. When death is all around the need to breed is at its strongest; that is in man's genetic makeup. My will was also subject to my genes I discovered. One afternoon outside the apartment a young girl of about sixteen came along the pavement. She had blondish, straight long hair and green eyes. The skin was almost, not quite, white. The body was fully developed and firmly curved, not that of a skinny pre-teen. She smiled widely at me as she came near. I drew a fistful of thousand franc notes from my pocket and held them out to her. She spoke only French and so we conversed in sign language; no talk was needed anyway.

The luxury of the apartment delighted her. The food and coffee were greedily consumed. The bath was gratefully accepted, filled with bubbles and put to long use. She came out wearing only the knee-length floral dress, carrying her underwear in her hand. She sat on my lap and my body began to switch to automatic drive. Just as I cupped her small, firm, pointed breast topped with erect nipple there was a long, loud knocking on the door. That was strange as knocking was not what we did; it should have warned me but balls were in charge. At the door stood one of the 51 Commando sergeants who, in retrospect, looked a bit sheepish and unsure of himself. My truck, he ordered, was to take five men to the outskirts of town to guard a road there and give early warning of an expected attack. My common sense was still in my pants. I signalled to her to wait, that I would be back soon; she nodded and blew me a kiss.

After four hours sitting on a road leading in to the city in the dark night the men on the truck had enough and demanded to go back. My suspicion was by then full-blown and the drive back was fast. On getting back to the apartment she was missing. Forbes' apartment was down the corridor but there was no answer to my knocks and the door was locked. Days later, when passion and rage had cooled the nubile girl came out of his rooms as I left mine. She smiled and blew a kiss. I would have gone badly wrong for Forbes just then had I got hold of him. Before I got my hands on him it had become a joke in the group and my rage collapsed. My reluctance to cross the colour bar had not been as absolute as I had believed it to be. Sex is a powerful thing.

One afternoon, soon after arriving in town, orders were given for us to attend a funeral ceremony. Several men had been killed on that long drive to Stanleyville. During the drive the firing up front by ambushers had downed one or two mercenaries. On the long drive rumour to that effect had been rife, but those of us far back in the convoy did not know the truth. Later it was confirmed that at one rebel roadblock the armoured head of the convoy had shot up, a rebel lay next to the road pretending to be dead and when the softer trucks carrying troops arrived he leapt to his feet and emptied his sub-machine gun into the men in the back of one truck, then quickly vanished into the black night and jungle. Other men had been killed by random shots from the dark at intervals on the drive.

The firing party were raggedly dressed mercenaries in an assortment of uniforms. Most of them were drunk or smoking marijuana. Hoare made a speech that rang false, as usual, full of praise for courage and fighting spirit. He seemed to have a stock of them and each was similar. A priest from the local Catholic mission said prayers and blanket-wrapped bodies were rolled into a communal grave. A bit of earth was shovelled over the bodies, but then a sniper in one of the tall palms on the banks of the river zeroed in on the cemetery and a firefight broke out and we scattered. The grave was left to be filled on another day. Who the men buried in that faraway cemetery were is still a mystery to me. They were fellow mercenaries but remain anonymous.

It was in Stanleyville that Aussie joined our little unit. He was a red-haired, squat, muscled man and being Australian was naturally called Aussie. He drifted away from his own Commando and fell in with me, Boeta and Harry. Harry had travelled the world widely, as had the Australian, and they and had once been in Nepal together for a few days. This was just another travel adventure for them both, a learning. Aussie was very aware of all that went on, and was very street smart. The trunks full of worthless Congo money still travelled with the Commando. Aussie waited until one of the Stanleyville banks reopened and then deposited all the funny money he could get his hands on in an account he opened. Maybe, he said, the country would recover and the money become worth something one day. In later years I often wondered about that money. My tin trunk full was thrown out into a street shortly before leaving the country. Aussie loved explosions, the bigger the better and he loved lots and lots of beer.

Aussie and I often went up to the roof of the apartment block where he set up a medium mortar and neatly laid out fused and boosted bombs. Directly opposite on the other side of the river was the port which, like a seaport, had overhead travelling cranes and railway lines all over the dockyard. There were steel-sided and blunt-nosed tugs like those used at sea docked near the cranes. This city was at the end of the navigable part of the Congo River. A short way upstream rapids spread across the river and blocked any further boat traffic. The docks were once a busy terminal. Sporadic fire by heavy machine guns and artillery still came from the dock area across the river, but the rounds fired were far off target; even our vantage place on the roof did not show where the rounds fell. Aussie sat next to the mortar tube with binoculars and waited until he located the source of the enemy fire and carefully sighted his mortar and fired. He danced a little jig when he scored a hit. It was all a deadly, remote-controlled game.

It was at one such roof session with Aussie when a sniper, way out on top of one of the dock cranes continually fired a rifle. The crack of the bullets and rifle could just be made out as a distant pop-pop. The sniper was ant-like in the steel structure and the sights of my FN slid to the 600-metre mark for a prone shot. After a long, careful aim I lifted the barrel higher and fired a single shot. Many seconds later the man in the gantry jerked and fell and then tumbled down the laced-steel structure to the rails beneath. It was a complete and perfect fluke, but Aussie could not stop dancing with glee and pumping my hand. To have measured the distance of that shot would have given me prime boasting rights, but it was never done.

About a week later an attack on the opposite shore was planned by Hoare and company. Half the city of Stanleyville was built across the river. Persistent information that an unknown number of nuns and other white people were still held hostage across the river had been around long before the convoy arrived. To have been effective the attack should have been mounted at once. Forbes had suggested to Hoare that 51 Commando conduct the attack on the first day, but was turned down without explanation. Each day's delay further sealed the fate of the hostages. The 51 Commando offer had not only been concerned for the hostages. There was a pristine looting ground, open to any unit who crossed the river. Now, much too late for the hostages, a rescue attack was mounted. 51 Commando were finally given the job. Two tug boats, steel-hulled and fast, were brought in to transport the assault. The tugs' skippers had been press-ganged into taking the attacking force across the river. Both were terrified but the steel hulls were thick enough to withstand even large-calibre bullets, so they were reasonably safe.

Ten 75mm recoilless rifles were set up along the route. Heavy .50 machine guns, tripod-mounted, were brought up and joined the light artillery. Two twin-engined fighter-bombers from the air force, which had been recently brought into action, patrolled overhead. Both planes were armed with multiple machine guns and air-to-ground rockets. Hoare was in his element. This was D-Day all over and he was in sole command. At the appointed time a barrage was let loose on the enemy bank and mercenaries charged across the river, crouching behind the thick steel plating of the tugs. The aircraft strafed the far shore with rockets and machine-gun fire. The only danger for the tugs was from friendly fire. Some of that came very close before the shore barrage stopped and the planes were left alone to cover the landing area ahead of the tugs. Not a single shot was fired from the enemy-held side.

The tugs docked and the mercenaries ran for the cover of the buildings at the back of the docks. All was silent and deserted. The Commando patrolled carefully along the road towards buildings further away from the dock area, on the watch for any movement or opposition. Fear levels are always high when the unknown is close. At one the end of the docks, where the jungle started was a native village of thatched pole huts and as the patrol went past a young boy about ten years old ran out of one of the huts and charged blindly at the patrol with a long panga. Instantly sickened with expectation I turned my eyes away. Shots boomed and the patrol went on. That the boy had been in a blind panic and that he did not know what he was doing charging at armed men was obvious. Was it not obvious to the other men? Could I have done anything to save him?

Later there was some talk the lad might have been one of the feared and legendary *jeunesse* but that was doubtful. The panic was clear to see, but as he was armed he was shot down. After half an hour's walking the patrol found the church where the hostages were said to be and some of the men went in. The hostages, all of them nuns and priests, had been machine-gunned in the aisle and lay in a bloody, tangled heap. The blood was dry and the bodies bloating. The rescue was days too late. The patrol roamed the streets with revenge in mind but all was deserted. The Commando then moved to a roofless house near the docks to brew tea inside the protection of the windowless walls. Two fast cabin cruisers came over the river and the dead were loaded and moved across for burial in the grounds of the cathedral the other side of the river. There was a large and very old graveyard at the cathedral.

Time began to drag while we waited for the recrossing and adrenaline was still high. Some men explored the docks and discovered a diesel-shunting engine on the dock rails in working order and it was started up without trouble. The engine was joy-ridden up and down the railway, the river end of which had a buffer made by curled-up rail ends meant to protect trains from the edge. Below the buffer, moored at the dock, was a large, open steel barge. The engine was run back two hundred metres and everyone except the driver got off. The engine was put in gear and the throttle opened wide. As it gathered headway the driver leapt off. The engine struck the buffer and smashed through; crashed over the dock end where it mashed through the barge bottom with ease and both machines vanished into the depths.

Satisfied for the moment the men went to the river along a footpath and bathed in the swift black current. It was upstream from the oil leaking from the recent wreck. As the sun set crimson the steel barges were boarded for the return to the other side. At the apartment the meal was pork and beans. So ended Hoare's D-Day, which turned out to be a senseless expenditure of ammunition and effort, a prime example of not making use of the available advice. If 51 Commando had slipped swiftly across the river on the day of their arrival it is very likely the hostages could have been saved by a flying attack. All the signs were the priests and nuns had been shot a day or so before the attack finally arrived. By the time the massacre took place the mercenaries had already been in the city for many days.

After the big attack across the river, air-ground support cover by the newly arrived aircraft continued. Although Puren had recruited pilots at the outset, the promised planes were absent until that futile day. Now fighters began to fly cover for the patrols sent out on a regular basis to clear the district round the city. Any rebel ambushes on the side of the road were easy to see from the air. The B-26s would climb on sighting an ambush to thousands of feet and then go into a vertical dive firing all eight machine guns (four each side of the nose) and at the last moment trigger one or more 16-round rocket pods. The sound was like heavy thunder following a lightning strike. There was not much left of the small ambushes after one of those overkill attacks.

When elements of 5 Commando Group left the heavy central jungle for the more open country further north the air cover went along. The aircraft were in air-to-ground action over our patrols several times. The air cover left everyone feeling somehow cheated. There was two-way radio contact with the pilots and Boeta often asked them to just inform us of the ambush position and leave us to deal with it. The pilots were enjoying themselves too much to agree.

The city of Stanleyville was once a fairly big, modern city in the European style. Multi-storeyed, modern, glass-sided buildings covered the commercial sector. Lining the wide river were row on row of luxury apartment blocks and houses which had once belonged to the rich. The best, biggest houses were on the high ground near the mighty river. These fine houses had been looted of all that could be prised loose and carried away and doors and windows gaped empty. At every town the Commando came to, there was the same destruction. Two or three waves of looters over two or more years had destroyed the once up-market housing, almost totally.

The local tribesmen did not to want to live in big, European houses; only very few big-shot politicians and soldiers did. The upkeep was too high for people with no money or maintenance skills. When the whites left them empty, locals were content to live in grass huts as they had always done, or in the warrens of matchbox houses in the poorer areas they had become accustomed to. In Stanleyville, and the other towns, there had been no civic services in place since independence and black rule. Blistering buildings were un-painted and broken windows unrepaired. Everywhere the jungle reclaimed open space. That jungle was a living, hostile organism, designed by nature to rid earth of the virus called man.

In Stanleyville there was almost no traffic when the town was first reclaimed from the Simba. The military and the UN vehicles were the only ones on the road. The roads were full of very large and deep pot-holes. Outside of the urban centres no maintenance had been done on un-tarred roads, which received heavy rain for most of the year. The rural roads were not usable except with a four-wheel drive vehicle. Everywhere in the Congo hung an air of rotting decay in the towns; paint peeling, rubbish in heaps, road systems collapsing. The smell of rotting vegetation and buildings was reinforced by the smell of numerous old and new corpses. Rotting bodies, skeletons and bones littered the pavements and roads where people had been killed.

The European mercenaries of 6 Commando included many who professed the Catholic faith. They, like the Simba rebels, needed some juju in times of peril. One morning coming back from patrolling the outskirts of the city our unit fell in with two trucks of 6 Commando Group. On the back of one truck was a truly massive black man. He looked like a champion body builder. The small convoy drove along the road running next to the river and stopped where there was a steep drop-off. The bulky man got out, walked to the edge of the river and stood on the concrete rampart on the riverbank. Some of the 6 Commando Group men followed. The massive black asked them if he should move closer to the edge and was told he should. He shuffled forward right to the edge. At no time did he show concern or fear. Four men fired sub-machine guns on automatic fire. The big man was flung down into the fast flowing water and sank. That the magic water would protect him was his vain and dying belief.

As the ripples on the water vanished two Catholic priests arrived in a car and jumped out and questioned the men standing at the bank. The missionaries were at the time trying hard to stop the indiscriminate killing. The 6 Commando Group men denied loudly and fervently having done anything other than test-fire guns out over the wide river. The priests looked down at the water and saw nothing and left. Then the men involved in the execution all crossed themselves and kissed their fingers and pointed at the sky. Their own juju was the strongest. Such is the sad condition of man.

There was no measurable time, no dates and no calendars. One day 51 Commando were sent to a bridge on the outskirts of the city. A hydroelectric plant near the bridge powered parts of the city. A deep, fast concrete canal ran along the side of a tributary of the Congo, leading water in great volume to some hydro-turbines; amazingly the plant was still working. The Commando was also tasked to stop any attempted attack on the city by the rebels coming over the bridge. This was highly unlikely, so it is probable headquarters had become embarrassed by the visibility of so much indiscipline. The international press had arrived and it was time to hide the rabble.

So 51 Commando's own little convoy of two trucks and four Jeeps drove ten kilometres along a road lined by the matchbox houses of the poorer people of the city to the tributary and bridge. Just before the bridge another road ran along the tributary so that at the bridge was near a crossroads. A high bank on one side of the road had some buildings along the summit. A hundred metres back from the crossroads stood the small empty houses of the unseen and watching poor. The vehicles were lined up below the built-up bank and camp was made. The wide concrete canal with fast-flowing waters feeding the nearby turbines ran below the road next to the camp. The bridge spanned the cannel and tributary.

While my bed was in the cab of the truck, most of the Commando slept under the canvas covering the backs of the trucks. Further days of uncountable time passed with nothing happening and men inevitably got bored, needing adrenaline. There was a large zoo unseen across the bridge, from where lions roared day and night. Some curious men decided to cross the bridge and visit the zoo and set free the lions; they also believed there were maybe some edible animals to be found at the zoo. Being used to danger all the time men, like some physically abused women, need danger, in fact thrive on it.

"Listen, the only Simba across that bridge is a two-legged one," Boeta cautioned.

"Hey, you guys leave your watches with me, don't want them broken, won't sell that way," Harry chipped in.

Seven or eight mercenaries prowled in a double row across the bridge. The .50 Browning over the cab was facing the bridge and my instinct had me cock the gun and take the two grips firmly in hand. All that was needed was for my thumbs to push the safety buttons forward and my fingers to pull the trigger. Boeta climbed up and sat cross-legged on the roof with his rifle at the ready on his knees next to me. The patrol got to the end of the bridge where dense jungle began. Nothing happened so maybe we were wrong.

With the usual rapidity of an ambush being sprung, a storm of gunfire crackled madly in the quiet morning. Predictably the patrol had walked into an ambush. It was so obvious they looked stupid. For long seconds the forest echoed with gunfire and screamed curses. The heavy gun in my hands hammered out long bursts into the forest both sides next to the far end of the bridge. As the bullets screamed away the patrol members were reeling back across the bridge, some of them being half carried. Boeta stood on the roof of the truck and tried to pick out the enemy from the added height. Not a single sighting.

Three men had been wounded, one badly, having taken a shot gun blast in the chest. He was at once loaded for transporting to the airport, where Belgian Army doctors had established a clinic. European people shot or raped by the rebels and Congolese Army were treated there before being sent out of the country. There was not a single person in sight on the ten-kilometre drive to the airport along the road skirting the empty-looking rows of matchbox houses. The locals classified us as Congolese Army and so stayed well out of sight. Countless thousands lived in this massive, sprawling township and their presence could be felt if not seen. The wounded man was treated on the runway by doctors and put on a C-130 standing ready to leave. The man was lucky and, with all the timing in his favour, he eventually recovered in a South African military hospital. On the long drive back to the camp there was still not a soul to be seen in the dusty avenues among the glowering shacks. Thousands of hostile and hidden eyes watched.

✍

Two station wagons arrived one afternoon, driven by uniformed white soldiers speaking French. They paused at the camp briefly and then drove on and entered the nearby haunted shantytown. An hour later two of the soldiers arrived on foot from the shacks with a thin black man dressed in black trousers and white shirt and who was barefoot. The man was complaining long and loudly. The soldiers compelled him to sit down near our vehicles and then turned around and went back into the shantytown without giving us any information. The indignant black man continued to complain loudly, but no one understood what he was saying. He was speaking Lingala. His last misfortune was to find the mercenaries in a black mood. There had been no action and food was scarce.

"Hey, Harry. You speak frog, what is he saying?" I asked.

"No, man, it is not French. The bugger is giving me a headache. Wish he would shut up."

"Good idea. Watch this. Stupid Simba, you should have been quiet." Boeta got up and beckoned the loudly complaining man over. "Stand over there you dumb fucker." He pointed to the edge of the bridge and waved the man to stand there.

Pete, one of the Commando who happened to have been at school with me, but was two years junior, got up and went to join Boeta.

"Man, I don't believe that nutcase. Surely the bloke can see it coming?" Harry puffed blue clouds of smoke.

"Don't think they will do it, will they?" was my anxious comment.

Boeta and Ray suddenly put up their rifles and fired from the hip, on automatic, long bursts. The complaining man was smashed forwards and then lifted by them and thrown over the edge into the swift water below.

"Is that not better?" Boeta called. "No more fucking whining."

A while later the unknown white soldiers came back in the two station wagons. A few other blacks had been collected by them. One soldier got out, came to us and began to ask questions in French. Harry got up to interpret. A loud argument broke out. The French speaker stormed off in a rage. The two vehicles drove away with the soldiers gesticulating at us angrily. The identity of the men in the trucks was never revealed to us, but they could have been UN hired guards trying to protect UN personnel who had sent to repair the utilities of the town. It had been murder out of boredom; murder for fun. But it was also the result of a lack of communication and mistaken identity. The Commando had all assumed the man was a rebel captive.

"Hey, man, Boeta," Harry called, "you just wasted the power station engineer. Nice one."

"How the fuck was I supposed to know. Making too much fucking noise anyway."

"Remember Smiler, man; don't make a noise when Boeta is around."

Near the bridge a pile of sandbags had been placed in the centre of the crossroad, a small fort manned by three or four men. The sentry post commanded both roads each way for some distance. From it there was a clear view of several hundreds of metres up and down each road. One morning an armoured convoy of 6 Commando Group, the Belgian mercenaries, came from the town and went on up the road running along the riverbank. There was a brewery still functioning there somewhere in the distance; when everything else failed the breweries kept going. The convoy was made up of three Ferrets and two of the bathtub personnel carriers, all armoured against small arms fire. They waved and shouted greetings as they drove by in a cloud of dust. The column was gone most of the day and had all but been forgotten by late afternoon. The men at the sentry post were lolling on top of the bags playing cards. It was late afternoon; a red tropical sunset turned everything black.

The air was soon filled with the vicious hiss of bullets and chatter of multiple machine-gun fire. The majority of 51 Commando was at camp below the high ground and fortunately under cover from that fire. It was at once clear the incoming fire was from trained soldiers and not the usual opponents. It was concentrated and frighteningly accurate. The stuttering machine guns came rapidly closer and the Commando scrambled up to the lip of the bank to return the fire, shooting blindly as fast as possible through grass and trees.

Orders were screamed loudly in French and the firing stopped abruptly. The armoured column of the morning had found a plentiful supply of beer. They had spent the day drinking and loading crates to take away. The drinking made them forget 51 Commando was manning the crossroad. The lead Ferret had spotted the sandbags from a long distance in the red evening shadows. There were men sitting on them, black in the red glow of the setting sun, so it opened fire, accelerated down the road, moving to one side to allow another scout car to use its guns. Each of the sentries at the sandbags was hit. A fortunate three had flesh wounds, but another man had taken two bullets in the belly. His ripped and muddy intestines lay in the red dirt of the road.

A very heated exchange was shouted back and forth. Harry began to sidle towards the lead Ferret, the main culprit, with a grenade in each hand. The other Commando men moved to screen Harry's intentions but the driver of the Ferret, with his head popped out of the driver's hatch, noticed. His head withdrew, the hatch snapped and then the gunner also dropped down inside and slammed the top hatch. Boeta appeared in front of the Ferret with a bazooka on his shoulder; fearing for my own safety I leapt forwards and pushed the anti-tank's barrel down. If the armoured cars had fired on us at point-blank range there would be many dead. Time stood still until the two Ferrets accelerated away towards town followed by the rest of the column. Their machine guns tracked us until they were out of sight. How was it that I was still alive? What a sweet evening it was. Relief flooded over me in a tide of emotion.

The shot man was barely alive, and his eyes began to glaze. What to do? It seemed obvious that he would not survive. He was pleading softly for help. His entrails were pushed back into his stomach and a blanket was wrapped around his body to keep them in. Sergeant Ginger injected morphine, far too big a dose, but there was really no kinder option. The hurt man was loaded on the truck wrapped tightly in the blood-soaked blanket and Boeta came along with me on that long drive back to the Belgian Army field clinic at the airport. The now quiet man was handed over to the doctors. A doctor examined him quickly and said he was not fatally injured. Then his breathing and heartbeat were checked. What, asked the now angry doctor, had the man been injected with? Loads of morphine, we said, to ease his death. A highly irate doctor tongue-lashed us, and others nearby joined in. As it was in French we did not understand the words but the gist of it was easily grasped.

"Fuck me; you would swear I did the thing. Shit man, you and me, we took him to the doctors."

"No sodding justice ever is there?"

"Right, Smiler. Would have been better to put a bullet in his head. If he was my dog I would have done that. Fuck them anyway."

11

O rders came one day for a return to the city. It was an immense relief to leave that deserted, silent place where a thousand unseen eyes watched. Whether the lions were caged or loose on the other side of the bridge remained an unsolved question, as no one had attempted to cross again after the first ambush. Back at the city apartment I felt a subtle change came over me. Maybe the break from the violence in the city did it, or maybe I had adapted as men always do, but I was no longer afraid the whole day and night and relaxed a bit. Man becomes used to even extreme violence in the end. By now a firefight was not the confused and scary thing that it once was. When the shooting started it made sense to me and was not just a jumble of loud sound. What was dangerous and what was not became clear. Not being scared and tense all the time allowed me to leave my rifle behind for a while in the city; carrying a .357 Magnum revolver was ample protection from the minor dangers of the streets. Casual murder and mayhem had become normal everyday events which passed with hardly a notice.

51 Commando remained in Stanleyville for some weeks, but just how long is just a jumble of days. During that time the bar in the Hotel Stanleyville had been drunk dry and restocked several times. The hotel management, who were mixed-blood Greeks, were paid with Government requisitions they knew were useless, but were too afraid to reject. Did that grand old tin-roofed hotel make it to the end of the war; does it exist today? I would like to know, but I guess it is a crumbling ruin today. Each evening in the bar we were served pies, prawns and other such snacks alongside the free drinks. On New Year's Eve 1964 the festive dinner was presided over by Hoare and his staff who sat at the head table with the Swedish Ambassador and grand speeches were made. Nostalgia saw to it that most of the men stayed sober during dinner and only a few got into half-hearted brawls. We talked a lot of home and New Years past. While Hoare was standing with a glass in hand, his uniform neat and ironed and his twin badge beret just so on his head, I decided finally and clearly that he was a fraud, a hollow shell. My first impression had been right all along; he had all the right words and played a well-versed role like an actor on a stage.

In that same instant of clarity I also realized what fools we mercenaries were to have believed the money promised would, ever be paid. It was four months into the contract and two months to go and no payments could be confirmed. Greed had been the driving force and only motivation and it made us believe the big amounts we were promised would arrive. Later on that night, after the year had turned, with little fanfare and no dancing Harry, Boeta and I talked solemnly as drunken men do about money. Harry smoked his fragrant Dutch pipe tobacco, and talked with the stem of his pipe firmly clamped between his teeth and his Labrador eyes far-distant.

"Look, man, no sense in not going on to the end is there. Man, we must just keep on and hope. Our own men are now in the pay office. Some money must come, man."

"No fuck it, I'm going to find big loot," Boeta said angrily and the grey wolf eyes gleamed in the dim light.

"Me, I'm just tired, too sodding tired to give a fuck. How the hell did they make such a fool of me? But then I suppose I never really believed we would ever get paid. Doubted it all from the start; it is too much to hope for. It is like buying a lottery ticket. You dream about getting the money and being filthy rich but a part of you knows it will never happen."

We sat sipping our drinks in silence for a while.

"So man, you guys going on?" Harry asked anxiously. The adventure could not yet end like this as far as he was concerned.

"What choice is there?" I asked, feeling a hundred years old.

"Ja, well, I'm telling you guys something. Me, I'm going to do big time loot," Boeta said, the grey eyes widening in challenge.

A suspected case of rabies was reported over the festival season. Stray dogs all over town had been eating the numerous corpses rotting away on the pavements. So orders were given to shoot any dog on sight. There were two trained gun dogs at the hotel, well-trained dogs. They sat on order and whined when they saw the executioner aim. That killing was very hard for me to bear. It was because it did not matter when men killed men. Men were at war with each other. But the dogs had not asked to be involved and had caused no offence to anyone. I wished there could have been some other way. It was very sad and depressing shooting those two anxious, cringing dogs. The Commando had an accumulation of pets by then, mostly African grey parrots and small monkeys, but no one gave any thought to the possibility they too might be infected by rabies.

The skeletons and skulls were everywhere in the streets. This availability supplied the means for one of the more insane men to sell skulls to use as ashtrays to the Marines at the airport. A skull with an identifiable bullet hole in it fetched the best price. The demand for skull ashtrays grew so much that the nutcase rigged a drum over an outside fire and boiled clean partly rotted human skulls. A wire brush was used to remove any fragments still on the bones, and they were put in the sun to dry. The required holes were carefully shot in the right place with a pistol. When dollars could not be obtained for the skulls, he accepted chewing gum cartons or rations packs.

Imagine this: a dirty, wild-looking mercenary walking the runway below the parked transport planes with a row of skulls laced on a rope over his shoulders, and calling out, "Real rebel skulls, what am I bid? Boots, gum, dollars for a genuine Simba skull? Gimme dollars and they're yours. Gimme dollars or gimme gum. Simba rebels skulls. The real, genuine thing."

It was also in that festival, or the hiatus after it, that Boeta began to scout the town for his big payday, dragging a somewhat reluctant me along. 51 Commando was doing nothing and there were still no orders from above. We took one of the Italian Army-design Land Rovers with the armoured half-windscreens and twin FN MAGs. Looking for change I manned the guns and let him drive. Boeta had heard from Matahari, the spy, that there was a warehouse in this industrial area somewhere packed with ivory. He had in mind a scheme, the details of which he did not share with me, to sell the ivory. Boeta was not interested in clothing or similar stuff that was too bulky and of little sale value. He wanted valuables. The ivory story sounded to me much like the lost gold mines of Queen Sheba, but there was not much else to do. We drove through the deserted industrial section of the city, stopping at each building large enough to conceal an ivory horde. The streets here were also still deserted. The civilian population was still hiding in the forest or in the warrens of the matchbox houses on the outskirts of the city. Unseen eyes seemed to burn into the back of my neck as unseen guns aimed at me. It was easy to get jumpy in a deserted area of a city,

There was a long hangar-like tin-sheet-clad building in the one street and Boeta parked facing the big sliding doors, which were closed. He slung his FN over his shoulder and pushed the doors open and vanished inside. Watching alone from the Jeep behind the guns increased my unease. It was too quiet and deserted and the feeling of being watched very strong. Maybe a rifle was about to be fired with me as the target. My head swivelled quickly as my eyes looked at each building in sight. There came, suddenly with increasing loudness, the sound of running feet and a black man dressed in tattered shirt and trousers burst from the doors of the building. He was right on the Jeep when he saw it because he was looking backwards over his shoulder as he ran. Then he stopped and fell down in fright.

I was as scared as he was now, and the only thought in my mind was to kill before being killed. To swivel the guns downwards enough to shoot, the Jeep had to be reversed. In that slow suspended time of danger the required actions went by in a blur and the guns fired, then disgust and sorrow filled me, all in one instant. The act was done without conscious thought and now the man lay on the ground, dead and leaking blood from a dozen holes. The fresh blood smell drew the butterflies, first one and then more. If he was a Simba rebel he was not armed. Yet again fear drove me, fear that I thought I had conquered.

Boeta came out of the building and looked at the dead man. He gave me thumbs up. It turned out the man had been the guardian of a vast pile of ivory tusks in the building which Boeta did not want anyone else to know about. He was going to shoot the man himself. That is why he was running. In the otherwise empty building were several hundred tusks. Boeta wanted that information to be his exclusively. Ivory to him was far more valuable than some unknown black man. At least he had a reason. I had none for my actions.

We had previously looted carved ornamental tusks but they were too big to carry around and so became immune from looting. Boeta was now determined to make money out of the large ivory cache. He worked on it. At one of the afternoon sessions of poker with the American C-130 pilots he was put in contact with a charter plane owner, one of the hard characters who wander round the fringes of any minor war. His battered Skymaster cargo plane was for hire to the highest bidder. After long negotiations he agreed to fly the ivory to Dar es Salaam to sell to some Arab ivory buyers he knew. He agreed to take a quarter of the ivory as payment. The deal was done and Boeta recruited a labour gang at gunpoint from the edge of the city. Then at night loaded, what I estimate to have been, fifteen tons of ivory over three nights. That one massive deal made Boeta a lot of money and gave him reason to return on other contracts. My guilty conscience would not let me get involved, so I merely watched from a distance. My guilt was deep after killing the watchman and taking any of the money seemed to be wrong. Boeta could not understand my feelings and he was right to mock me. It made no sense.

It was at that idle time our mutual insurance group went over to 53 Commando, which was commanded by John Peters. 51 Commando had fallen apart owing to the complete lack of command. 53 Commando had been ordered to a city in the north of the country, Paulis, on a hostage retrieval campaign and the chance of loot was fairly good as the Belgian paratroopers had dropped on that town at the same time they came to Stanleyville and had been there in force for some weeks. Their presence would have stopped any looting. Arrangements were simply made by approaching Peters and getting him to agree to let us join 53 Commando.

Peters was an emotionally volatile man with a vicious temper. Like Boeta he had grey, almost white, wolf-like eyes, and had a long military career behind him. He had firm control of 53 Commando and was also very keen to find loot. The trip north was in a DC-6 which on the way hit a violent thunder storm so the plane was tossed about in the sky like a scrap of paper in the wind. The lumbering planes of that time seemed to be unable to get above the black clouds of tropical storms over central Africa and flew right through the worst of them.

Within days of our defection Peters showed his vicious side. It started the night before when the local cook for the Commando had been ordered to produce meat.

His pay was very high by local standards as it was in looted, useless, Congolese francs. It easily covered anything he was told to buy locally and still left him a fortune. Meat was scarce so a monkey went into the pot. The apes were sold in the market with hair burnt off on an open fire and tied up in a tight bundle. The stew was very tasty as we eaters did not know what the meat was. We were unaware until Peters forked a small hand with fingernails attached out of the mess on his plate. Most of the men laughed and carried on with the meal. Peters went white with rage, and threw the plate against the wall. The cook had already gone home.

The next morning the poor unsuspecting cook, chasing money like the rest of us, made the morning coffee and bread. When takingPeters his coffee, he happened to stumble, spilt the coffee and the cup smashed on the floor. Peters shouted for someone who could talk Swahili to tell the cook to take the saucer back and clean it. As the now trembling man went outside, Peters shot him in the back, ordering the body to be taken to the nearby jungle and left there.

ε∿

The town of Paulis had been attacked by a large convoy of Simba rebels, intent on retaking it some days after the Belgian paratroopers had arrived. The rebels drove towards town with a long convoy of trucks filled with armed men. The road they chose was cut dead straight and almost level through the forest for about ten or more kilometres. The Belgians soldiers had set up heavy machine guns and mortars on the roof of a tall building which overlooked that straight, wide road through the forest. The convoy was halted by sustained fire, bullets and mortars, and scores of rebels died on the trucks and on the road. It is hard to understand the stupidity of the rebels in these matters. They believed implicitly in the witchdoctor's spell which would turn bullets to water. But knowing that still induces disbelief. The burnt and wrecked convoy full of rotting corpses and had to be driven through on the way out of town. We did that trip many times and each time the foul air from the decaying corpses caused us to gag and vomit.

Road patrols out of Paulis had air cover that was supplied by the same types of aircraft which had covered the river crossing in Stanleyville. One was a small single-seater prop-driven plane similar to the old and lumbering Harvard from the Second World War. They were American-built and flown by pilots recruited by Puren, Hoare's right-hand man. Some of the pilots were from South Africa but most were anti-Castro Cubans. The small plane was armed with a machine gun on each wing. Then there were bigger fighter-bombers. They had twin engines, one each side of the cockpit on the wings. They carried eight .50 machine guns jutting from the nose and four pods of air-to-ground-rockets, two pods to each wing.

The smaller slow aircraft was designated a T-23 by the Americans and the more powerful, fast twin engine one the B-26. Both were Second World War vintage. Their guns and rockets were more than sufficient for any job they had to do, which was ground support, and carrying bombs in the B-26 was unnecessary. Two B-26 fighter-bombers had gleefully joined in wrecking the rebel column which tried to counter-attack Paulis. The rockets had shredded the trucks to scrap. The B-26s had come up with us from Stanleyville and they flew constant air cover for any patrol sent out of Paulis. Patrols went out every day.

Paulis was a pleasant little town built on gentle green hills near the Ugandan border. A few kilometres out of town the thicker rainforest gave way to rolling hills covered in green grass, with trees scattered like solitary animals over the plains. The forests surrounding the town were unlike the equatorial forest further south. The tall trees, much like giant redwoods, had park-like open land in between them, not the hot humid green tangle of the rainforests. It was coffee plantation country. It was farming country. But this is Africa, and again I often wonder what happened to those immense estates.

Some of the town's commercial businesses were intact; one of those was a big beer brewery. It had only been running for a short while, but for unknown reason was closed when we arrived. As the owners of other businesses were present, and had Belgian Army protection, we could not loot them. Aussie had come over with us to 53 Commando, and he was now rabid for beer.

We had taken over a large luxury house on the edge of town that had once belonged to the provincial governor. The electricity and water still worked and once the drain had been unblocked in the shower that also functioned. There we had the ultimate luxury of hot water showers. The afternoon after we installed ourselves, with most of us sleeping on the floor, which was hard, but at least it was out of the rain, we set off, led by Aussie, to search the brewery in the hope of finding beer.

Inside the brewery stood tall steel vats which, on inspection, appeared to be full of beer. The silvery steel vats looked like smallish grain silos. The massive hall was a confusion of pipes and machinery with empty bottles standing on conveyor belts and in massive pallets of wood. There seemed to be no simple way to get to the beer in the vats apart from breaking them open. Then Aussie revealed he had once worked in a similar bottling plant; one of hundreds of jobs he had done in his wanderings. He went about opening valves and flexible connection pipes. Suddenly beer squirted out at high pressure from a hose he was holding. Plastic buckets were rounded up and used to collect the gushing beer. The buckets were also used as drinking mug to quench our immediate thirst. By the time it was decided to return to the house much beer had been poured down eager throats. We carried many others litres back to the mess.

Peters, as commander, at once set to locating the factory staff. Then an arrangement was made with them to bottle the beer and sell it. Peters took a cut of all the profits and provided any strong-arm protection needed. Cases of beer were supplied to the mess as part of the deal, and the workers were allowed to take some home but most of the production was to be sold. A big stock of barley and hops was located in the complex and the press-ganged production staff managed to produce beer non-stop for all the weeks 53 Commando stayed in Paulis. Aussie was in his heaven and all was fine on his earth.

"So my mates, can I arrange a piss-up in a brewery or what?" was his comment on that drunken first day and it had all of us hooting with helpless, childish laughter.

One 53 Commando sergeant was a Scot called Sam. He used no other name. One buttery sunny morning Sam and I were on the way back to the mess after collecting beer, when we came across three Congolese soldiers carrying a chicken and prodding along in front of them a man who was obviously the owner. He had probably had the effrontery to protest when his precious chicken was taken and so was being taken off for execution. Forcing Sam to stop, I got out of the truck to save the chicken owner. It was a stupid, hasty decision and later I realized my emotion was surfacing which was not a good thing here in the Congo. There was no common language between me, the soldiers or their captive so things at once became difficult, confused and heated.

As always I carried my FN slung over my shoulder, but Sam, who had been driving the truck, was unarmed. Things became very heated and if I had less beer in me I would have backed off. The argument got to the stage where the three black soldiers began to bring their weapons to bear. The situation had boiled swiftly over and now was dangerous with possibly fatal consequences for me. Adrenalinee and rage slowed my world down and narrowed focus to the road and the men on it. Boeta and the armoured Jeep came into my peripheral vision. At once, understanding what was going on, he stopped and moved behind the twin MAGs. Then he shouted at the soldiers in fluent Swahili to stop and go away.

Above Boeta's loud orders came a shrill pleading from behind and on turning I saw the chicken owner lying on the ground pleading with me to stop the man standing over him from shooting. That soldier grinned and killed the man with a long burst in the back. More than any other thing in life right then I needed to kill that soldier but Sam pushed me back into the truck as Boeta covered the angry Congolese soldiers with the twin MAGs. There were high-ranking Congolese officers in town who could have ordered me executed if I had given full vent to my rage.

The triumphal, mocking shouts of the black soldiers echoed in my head as the truck drove away. During the fracas the chicken escaped and flew away over a fence. The owner now lay dead in the gutter from an act of sheer spite. Sam was angry; if

I had not attempted intervention maybe the man would be still alive. Sam had not seen the massed graves in Lisala and I had. It was the African way and white men should not have got involved was his opinion, as mine had been once. The incident, just another in the hundreds of similar, left an immense sadness in me. It was but one more needless death. Could the man's life have been saved is a question which is always with me.

Another incident came shortly afterwards, to prove that it was not only the black soldiers who had no respect for life. A rebel had been captured somewhere in town and circumstances brought him to one of our messes. 53 Commando had in it men who had come up directly from Kamina and had not seen any action. Sam drew his .45 automatic pistol and made ready to take the capture into the nearby forest for execution. The new men crowded eagerly forward. This was the chance they had been waiting for, to see how it felt to kill. To watch a man being killed, this was the biggest thing in life. Now they were about to find out about killing a man. Hindsight allows me to recall that, right then at the house on the edge of Paulis was the moment the idea there was indeed right and wrong began to bother me. Doubt about the right of killing that man made me step forward and hold up the proceedings. Sam looked at me with a question on his face.

"Are you sure he is Simba?"

"They got him in town with his gun. What else could he be?"

"Hang on." The problem was again not being able to speak Swahili. I pointed to the totally unconcerned men "Wewe Simba? Wewe Mulele?."

"Eh-he," He tapped himself with a finger. "Simba, Simba."

"That seems to be very clear. Are you happy, Smiler? What with you suddenly liking the wogs anyway, hey?"

"Ah, fuck it Sam. Do it." I turned away defeated and the new men crowded in and pushed the man towards the trees.

A while later came a ragged volley of shots. When they returned from the execution the new men looked very shaken and white. The death of a man, especially shot in cold blood, always has a sobering effect on watchers. The sudden drop and finality of it hits hard. I was suddenly very worried about the new emotion, one that had me querying right and wrong; the emotion that pushed me to try for justice on the road with the man and his chicken and now again with the capture. It worried me at the time as it was a recipe for disaster in the existing environment.

The purpose of sending 53 Commando to Paulis had been to gather the Europeans still left on the many farms and plantations in the area, and bring them to safety for eventual evacuation. The area had not been attacked or devastated by the rebel forces, who had by-passed it on their way south; it was the Congolese Army now arriving, and they made it advisable for all Europeans to leave. Many othe white refugees elsewhere had been brutally attacked by the Congolese Army over the last few years. The black government had no objection to all whites being driven out of the country. Though it was not an officially stated policy the troops on the ground carried it out as if it was. The Government was supported by the Americans, who were easily mollified by the assurance that atrocities were isolated incidents. The black soldiers were used to raping, killing and looting as a right and whites were their preferred victims.

So mercenary patrols went out from Paulis to search the area. This was done in the usual group of two Jeeps with eight men. It was easy work because the gravel roads were in relatively good condition as it did not rain as much as in the jungles further south. It was also quite different country for the rebels as it was very difficult to set an ambush in this open rolling grassland, unlike the forests further south. Any ambush set near the road would need to be done in a very professional manner not to be seen by the approaching vehicles. There was only short, green grass growing each side of the good wide roads. The rebels did not have the required military skill. The ambush, to be hidden, had to be far off the road.

Day after day the many coffee estates and large farms were searched. No Europeans were found by the Commando. Coffee trees lined the roads, the red berries heavy and waiting for harvesting which would not come. The estate buildings stood empty and deserted. Houses and sheds on the plantations had been looted, probably by the abandoned labour force. All the whites had already gone, leaving behind their dreams and hopes and a lifetime of work. We could not find anyone to rescue.

Yet at odd times in Paulis small convoys of Europeans arrived in town and were sheltered by the Belgian Army and military air transport to Europe was arranged for them. They looked just like refugees of 1960, who had camped at the Salisbury show grounds and earlier driven past the hall at Kitwe where we Territorials watched in dismay. How many broken dreams and shattered lives had countries like the Congo produced in only a few years of black rule? Tens of thousands of lives ruined and tens of thousands killed. Why? The only possible answer was racial hatred; the blacks were killing because they hated the whites. But that does not begin to explain the thousand of blacks killed by other blacks in recent years in Africa. If there is any one answer it is very elusive.

The daily patrols without action meant boredom quickly set in. The aircraft prowling overhead ensured the vehicle patrols were not ambushed. There was just the daily grind of driving many kilometres out and then back to the small town and settling down to drink beer. But there was sometimes comic relief. One member of the Commando bought a full-grown chimpanzee from one of the departing plantation workers. It was very human and ate cereal in the morning from a plate with a spoon. It also had a taste for beer and would sit at the table and pour the bottle into a glass and drink it. Things got messy after the chimp had too many beers. It also had a taste for sweet things and knew when the nuns at the nearby mission baked cakes or biscuits. When he smelt the baking the ape sneaked off to the mission and rampaged about the kitchen till the nuns locked themselves in another room. Then the ape snatched loot unhindered and came back hooting triumphantly, face covered in icing and both hands and mouth pouches packed. It also took a liking to firing the machine guns mounted on our vehicles. It did a small jig and hooted wildly each time the gun fired.

Each Jeep carried a bazooka anti-tank weapon which fired armour piercing rockets. A box of two shells was packed in a wooden box kept with the tube. The weapons had never been used in the role they were made for. Ours had been turned into containers for beer and ice. The weapon's tube folded in two and each half had caps fitted to keep the tubes clean. Ice and beer bottles fitted well into each capped half. On that particular sun-drenched day the gravel road ran along the rolling hills for kilometre after kilometre. It was like riding a gentle roller-coaster, up and down in endless sweeps. From the top of one hill only the top sections of the following hills were visible and not the valley between as the road gradient was fairly steep. In the weeks of patrolling these plains that stretched from horizon to horizon there had been no other traffic on the roads.

As usual I drove the leading armoured Jeep with Boeta behind the twin machine guns and Harry in the back seat leaving a blue trail of smoke in the still air behind the Jeep from his pipe. As we crested a hill and began to go down into the following valley a tank came into sight. It turned out to be a light tank but at first sight it was very big and menacing. The tank's main gun fired and a shell screamed overhead, missing and exploding against the next hillside. In a total panic both Jeeps skidded to a halt. Harry scrambled about behind us, cursing loudly, trying to quickly empty the bazooka of beer bottles and at the same time to smash open the wooden shell crate. Another shell screamed overhead and again there was a distant explosion.

Boeta began firing both machine guns together at the tank; the others crouched next to the Jeeps, which gave no cover at all from shell fire, firing rifles in a fury. The second Jeep had stopped further back up the hill and also fired with all guns on the tank. The rounds could be heard ricocheting off the steel sides of the metal monster, the strike of the bullets leaving nothing but small marks on the green paint. As the rocket for the bazooka was being fumbled home by Harry, who was by then lying in the road, the hatch of the tank flew open and the crew of four jumped out and tried to run away. Before they had gone ten paces they had all had been hit multiple times by bullets. They were cut to pieces; parts of heads, arms and legs fell off, such was the fury of our concentrated fire.

The tank was six-wheel-driven and had a diesel engine, heavily armoured at the turret and all round the hull, with a .303 calibre machine gun firing from the turret alongside the 2-pounder main gun. It was later identified as a British-made and the speculation was that it had once been in use in British-run Uganda. The border was not far away, just to the north of the incident. What was a mystery to us was why the crew had abandoned it to meet certain death. It was in perfect order, as the storm of bullets had hardly scratched the paint.

We put one of our men inside, closed the hatch and again fired at the tank from close by. From inside the sound of the rounds striking the hull was deafening, like a bucket on your head being hit by hammers. The inexperienced black crew had taken fright at the sound of the bullets striking. That was the only conclusion we could come to. The fuel tanks were full and the engine ran sweetly so it came back to Paulis at the van of our two Jeeps. It became the vehicle used in front of all future patrols. Boeta always loved to ride in the front of any convoy. Now he rode the tank. He sat on the outside of the hatch with his thighs locked around the main gun, eagerly looking for a target ahead. Luckily for him the tank did not go into action while he was perched there on the main gun.

Paulis was a little different to the other towns of we had been in. Some commerce was still going on. A few locals walked the streets. The presence of a strong unit of the Belgian Army, who had no time for the rapacious Congolese Army, had saved a lot of the town from wanton destruction by them and us. There were no unburied corpses or skeletons in the streets which, by contrast, made the destroyed convoy just out of town worse. It was a normal, once-prosperous, colonial settlement, only here there were no white settlers left. The solid neat houses where white people had lived for many decades stood empty. Many houses looked as if they were locked up while the owners were away on holiday; but the owners would never be coming back. The same feeling came to me in Paulis as it had in every ruined town; the jungle was busy taking back its own. Only here outside Paulis the jungle was not thick and humid. It seemed more patient, advancing at a slower pace. The big trees and undergrowth would be slower to reclaim than the fetid green rainforest.

The contract was near an end and still no money had been paid into our bank accounts back home. There was another meeting with Hoare and his headquarters staff and yet again the only suggestion they had was to put new men in the paymaster's office. This time our delegation sent to the pay office threatened death to all and sundry if the pay was not forthcoming at once. The men sent were chosen to ensure the threats would, this time, certainly be carried out and those in the pay office soon knew that. The plan, and the threats, finally worked as just days before the end of the six months news came that some monies had been paid. If those payments had not then been made there would certainly have been killings. The men now watching the paymaster had been through a lot for the money and were determined to kill the next man who stole their pay. Certainly any man foolish enough to do so would have been hunted down wherever he went in the world. It was all about the money. Nothing else mattered.

Once the remnant of sad, ragged whites had been cleared from the estates and plantations and sent to Europe, and the area left to the mercy of the Congolese Government, there was a lot more time on our hands. The killing had long stopped and the bones of the dead cracked in the sun and rain. The rain washed the stench of rotting flesh away; nature slowly groomed and cleaned the mess made by man. The lack of daily adrenaline led to withdrawal symptoms which caused the men to seek substitutes for the daily diet of action and death. Danger and adrenaline is a hard, addictive drug. Those who had been in the Congo for a while were hooked.

All boys like to play with weapons. Few men are given the chance to indulge that urge to the full but we now found there was an oversupply of ammunition and explosives. Great efforts had been made to stock up on all munitions in anticipation of further daily fighting which had never occurred. The rebellion had drifted away from this part of the country and centred on the Great Lakes region, where it festered for decades, the fighting there dragging on right up until today. The fighting has a base in tribal lands divided by white proclaimed borders. Warlord versus warlord in tribal land disputes keeps the Congo the murder and rape capital of the world.

With heavy machine guns, an assortment of sidearms, many different types of grenades and mortars, and some heavy ordnance like the 75mm recoilless anti-tank gun in abundance, it was hard to resist the urge to play. We loaded a couple of trucks and drove off to the deeper forest near town. The towering trees were growing in fairly thin undergrowth and the biggest of them were selected as targets. For hours on end a variety of weapons were fired at will. The detonator in the shells from the recoilless guns was set to explode at different intervals after striking the target. The prime object was to have the detonation take place inside the trunk of the massive tree. That way the tree was felled and the mighty creaking crash was awe inspiring in the immensity of destruction it caused. The cough of heavy machine guns and grenades exploding went on for hours and above all was the delighted shrieks of laughter reminiscent of a school playground.

A long, straight road ran out of Paulis past the mission station, and it went down a long valley and then up a distant rolling hill. On each side of the road there was light forest and there were some oil palms nearer town at the start of that road. To the left of the road was a collection of rusting car shells. The roadside forest had once been used by a long-gone garage workshop as a dumping ground for unrepairable vehicles. A pair of recoilless rifles was set on tripods at the top end of the road and we practised firing rounds at the rusty car shells. A van carrying nuns from the mission arrived and the ladies got out and watched. They were in their white cloaks but with uncovered heads. The guns fired rocket-assisted shells and the full might of the rocket blast exited the back of the barrel; the blast made matchwood of a wooden shell crate left to demonstrate it. The nuns were intrigued and persuaded the mercenaries to allow them to load, aim and fire the gun.

Aim was made through optic sights which distorted nearby objects. One nun twisted open the breech and pushed in a shell, the other knelt at the side of the gun and looked through the sights, spinning the aiming wheels to centre on one of the distant car hulks. The barrel swivelled to her aiming commands at the wheels. The nun gripped the trigger handle and pushed the tit. The rocket roared out, the blast whooshed and the high explosive round hit a nearby palm. The optics had distorted the palm in the aiming lens. The explosion was ear-shattering and two of the Commando at the side of the road near the nuns fell down wounded by steel shrapnel. One man had a minor chest flesh wound, the other a hole the size of a fist over his kidney and the steel shrapnel scrap could be seen inside his body cavity. The hurt man had immediate attention and was, an hour later, flown to South Africa by the Belgians. The nuns were mortified and could not stop apologising.

"Oh man, oh man, no one will anyone ever believe him when he tells them the story of his wound," Harry giggled, "I mean man, shot by a nun, man, playing with an anti-tank gun?"

Aussie found a crate of gun cotton, small square blocks of stable explosive ignited by inserting a detonator cartridge in a small hole in the block. His love of big bangs had no outlet in the now quiet town. His mortar tube had seen little use recently and he needed a big bang. There was a solid brick house near the one we used as a mess. It had a tin roof on wooden rafters. The doors and windows were gone but there was a wooden table in one room in the middle of the house. Aussie found wire for an electric detonator by pulling out the electrical wiring from the house, about twenty metres when it was all linked. Then Aussie got his hands on a still live 9-volt radio battery and all was ready to make a big bang. The gun cotton was taped to each of the legs of the table and each bundle linked with Cordtex.

"Watch this mate. Will it fly or what, mate? I reckon it will, mate, like a giant bird."

"Well, man, it might fly but you will too with that short wire, "Harry grinned, puffing out blue smoke.

"Hey, Aussie, that is a big charge of gun cotton. One block will be enough to blow that house up."

"Not on, my mate Smiler, like it must fly, not explode, fly like a giant bird. Right?"

The rest of us backed off a hundred metres and left him to do his thing. Aussie went inside and carefully placed a silver detonator in the first bundle of gun cotton. Then he backed away gingerly to the outer extent of the wire. Looking up he grinned and gave us a thumbs-up. Carefully he touched the battery to the wires. With a typhoon roar the explosive detonated in the house. It flew alright. The entire house rose from the foundations in one complete piece, just for a brief second, and then things went haywire rapidly. The building began to expand, driven up and out by the massive charge. The roof and rafters lifted, the walls bulged and then broke into flying bricks that shot in all four directions. The roof went up higher and then the tin sheets separated from the wood of the rafters and flew still higher. The twirling roof sheets went up and up, hundreds of metres into the blue sky. Then they began to fall and as they gained pace on the way down they began to spin, each sheet turning into a gyrocopter blade that swirled it far across the sky in ever-increasing circles above our heads.

"Fuck me, Aussie, give some warning so I can leave town next time," panted Boeta after we had stopped running and dodging the falling plates.

"Maybe next time you listen, hey, Aussie?"

"Whoooo, mates, that was a bit of alright."

"Hell, man, you put my pipe out." Harry complained.

"You are all OK, my mates, right dinkum." Aussie beamed, pleased with the day's work.

The end came swiftly and in the distorted time of no hours I suffered another terror-filled trip on an ancient Dakota across the purple stormy sky of Central Africa and after a lifetime landed back at Kamina. There was a vague regret in me; how stupid that lust for money had been; it brought me so much terror and ugliness, and it had been a futile little war. Mobutu negated any democratic effect the mercenaries might helped bring to the region by declaring himself President for Life, supported by his brutal army. Tshombe, who had wanted democracy, was eventually exiled and later murdered. His death was documented by the media. There were no headstones or news reports to mark the death of thousands of others in the steamy forests and in the wide black rivers. Never again was my vow, never again would I do something so stupid; yet deep down it stirred a sense of having become a man, a true hunter and predator, a feeling which is hard to come by.

Again it was a hot, blue and gold tropical day and the lumbering plane flew through disturbed weather to Leopoldville. Days were lost in the mist of time and alcohol spent in that sewer of a city waiting for another fear-filled flight to Johannesburg. Harry, Boeta and I quartered in a rat- and shit-filled hotel where the toilets overflowed into the corridors. The time spent waiting was a continual binge of whiskey, all day and night drinking whisky, mainly in one of the bars that were the main commerce of the city. Whisky was the only decent liquor, except for local beer, and the bars accepted the local money for it.

Money was plentiful as there were still many thousands of useless francs left over, our pockets still stuffed full. Boeta also had access to a local bank account and plenty of mighty America dollars, courtesy of the ivory deal. In the dark, beery bar he rolled dollars into a wad and put the wad in my and Harry's top pockets. The Blue Note was a nightclub in the capital still frequented by Europeans and it served reasonable food. All the hazy nights and most of the lost days were spent in the dark air-conditioned room that reeked of sweat and sex. The painted white prostitutes avoided us like snakes. They did not interest me, but there were other women in the Blue Note but they were visibly scared, and trying to bed them failed totally. They were sophisticated adult white women and I badly needed urgent sex so I tried hard. My unwashed state was not all that noticeable in the reeking room, but they all shied away when I got too close, like horses rearing back from a snake.

At that time the few remaining whites in Leopoldville kept out of sight as much as possible, kept to their own small enclaves. It was not advisable for white people to take part in public life, not advisable to become too visible. The few who hung on, some to this day, in the capital did so because they had sufficient funds to bribe all the many it was necessary to bribe to get on in any way. The senior government officials sniffed out anyone who had funds and at once extended a hand, offering protection or threatening arrest. Any white arrested had to pay a number of people from the warders to the chief of the prison to secure release. There were no law courts, only police. The whites remaining in the city were making a lot of money, as is always the case when there is chaos. Old hands in Africa always keep well below the radar.

A few businesses were still stumbling along in the decaying city, still trying to keep going after the Belgian pull-out three years back. One such shop offered clothing and there they fitted me with a safari suit made of Hessian, the long jacket worn outside the pants. It was sacking cloth lined with silkier material; sackcloth and ashes I thought fitted me well. Maybe the lining was curtaining from a looted house. Also some sandals, the flip-flop type, which were all that fitted my feet. We had been forbidden to wear any uniform onto the plane out.

Then a red giant of sun rose in the orange sky through the mist of the river and forest and we were eating something in a tatty café which opened day and night. The owner was a Greek and he was bleary-eyed from lack of sleep and unshaven. Boeta had a hangover and was also drunk, both at the same time, as we all were. The Greek was arguing loudly with a black waiter over some petty matter. The Greek called the waiter a Simba, in anger and for the benefit of the mercenary customers. The argument caused Boeta's wolf eyes to widen, then narrow, and the soft mouth to firm and pout. His automatic pistol came out held hidden behind his back.

"Are you a Simba," he said softly, standing up and grabbing the tribesman waiter by the ear.

"Yes, I am, and so is he," said the waiter speaking Swahili. "That Greek man he is a Simba."

"Me a Simba!" shouted the stubble-chinned Greek in English for our benefit. "You Simba!"

"Are you a Simba," Boeta asked again in a soft voice, his eyes dead.

"If that man says so then I am. Me Simba, you Simba," he shouted shrilly.

The pistol came up and the barrel stuck in the waiter's ear. The shot was muffled and blood and brains sprayed from the exit wound and splashed the wall and roof. There was general scramble for the door as the Greek tumbled behind the counter and vanished. He was screaming very loudly.

It was too much for me in my drunken haze. In a blind rage at the enormity of it all, I began to rise and reach for the .357 Magnum Colt on my own belt. This had to come to an end; it was too, too much. There could be no more of it. Kill the man and put a stop to it all. It must stop. How dare he cause me such agony.

Harry reached over the table and pushed me down with a heavy hand on my shoulder. "Live. Live, man. We came too far, too far to die now. Live is all we need to do man. Stay alive. Look, it too will pass."

My body slumped and the revolver slipped back to the holster. Boeta was standing looking towards the screaming man behind the counter. He had not noticed my actions. Suddenly a change like an awakening came over him, he shuddered and shook and blinked, and he put his pistol away slowly. He kicked the dead waiter softly.

"Fucking stupid shits, have always got to make a fucking noise. They never tell the truth, never. Come on you guys. Finish your coffee, let's find a quieter place. What about the Blue Note, the day shift will be on?"

The moon came up bright blue, silver and massive over the river and the water turned to black gold, reaching out to the blacker forests and the massive sedan might have been a taxicab. Three Congolese girls of about twelve were in the back compartment with us. They hiked short skirts and removed panties and one after the other mounted Boeta's cock as he lent back. The space was filled with sucking, moaning and sighs. One girl got down on the floor between Harry's legs and slowly moved her mouth up and down on his cock, and he lent back and sucked his pipe in unison with her mouth, blowing smoke from his nose, his sad eyes watching her head. A hand felt for me but my body did not respond, the whisky haze had disconnected my brain, and with it my sex drive. The need for sex surging strongly through my soused imagination but the impulse did not reach my groin and the hand went away with a giggle.

The furnace of the blood-red sun again in the moist orange sky and American Marines herded us like sheep towards an aircraft. There were doll-like painted hostesses on board and they ignored us as we drank direct from the neck of the whiskey bottles we had boarded with. There were very few other passengers on the Air Sabena jetliner but those few turned their faces away, injured. A few hours later and still drinking we were on the runway in Johannesburg and three men in blue and green safari suits, knee-high stockings and rubber shoes, all wearing identical pencil moustaches and lightly tinted brown glasses, ushered us with half-raised arms to a tin shack on side of the runway. There, fat Xhosa women served tea and sandwiches. Because of the chlorine, the tea tasted like swimming pool water, long alien to our taste.

With the dark glasses reflecting the noon sun the men shooed us towards a BOAC airliner bound for London, and passengers in evening clothes moved between the seats as ours were allocated. The three seats we were given were widely separated and for the first time in months we were out of sight of each other. Aussie had vanished somewhere sometime on the mean streets into a Congolese bank. On my lap was the toilet bag, companion of the long, dangerous roads travelled. In it was the small ivory palm tree, together with used-up toothbrush and a scrap of soap. My manners were knocking on the edge of the drunken haze and a blush burnt on my cheek as the hostess leant over and then recoiled, without helping to fasten my seatbelt as she had intended. The short flight to Salisbury could not be over soon enough and the stares of amusement and disgust from the other passengers reached me through the alcohol haze but I looked away at once.

The compulsory loud American who travels on every international flight was across the corridor. There was a far whine of jet engines and a steep rush into the clouds, drifting smoothly through the stars. The air conditioning circulated cool air. The Yank stood up and loudly sniffed that air, looked down at me sitting hunched and trying to be small.

"Jesus Christ, where the hell have y'all been?" he bellowed and some passengers clapped.

Epilogue

The first shock as I drove home was how clean that colonial town of Salisbury was, and everything worked, everything was neat and clean. Then the newly hardened soldier had to move back home with his mother. It was very strange that a few months had coloured my perception so much that everything normal felt strange and alien. There was some status to be had from being known as an ex-mercenary, but that did not last long, and in reality my qualifications were minimal. The reason for all the killing, the money, finally arrived and it was enough to live on for some time. At opening time, 10.30 each morning, the ex-mercenaries gathered in the Palace Bar in First Street, Salisbury. In the evening we all went to one of the nightclubs. Harry and Boeta had rushed through the airport on landing as I had, and now we met up again. It was not the same. Boeta went back to the Congo shortly afterwards for several more contracts. Harry went home to Canada after his father died and he inherited some money. We remained friends, but there was now no reason to watch each other's back and we were no longer close by necessity.

The money sent to the account was one month's danger pay of some £170. Several months after that a month's pay of £480 arrived; that money was more than a year's pay in a normal job. What happened to the rest of the money owed remains a mystery, but now back in civilization it became unimportant and nothing but a distant and greedy dream. What there was would not go far if each day was spent in the bar and every night in a nightclub. It was very soon that the company of drunk, boastful men wearied me. Those who saw little or no action were the loudest and most obnoxious. It was better to withdraw from them before all the money was gone, spent on nothing. There was no point in hoping for any more of the promised money. It was time to move on with a normal life.

One day an advertisement for recruits to the British South Africa Police caught my eye and without thinking too much I applied. The advertisement showed a man riding a horse on patrol in the bush. That was what I yearned for: the peace of the vast, clean and friendly veldt that had raised me. Like all advertisements that one was also puffery. The next 16 years of my life was in the British South Africa Police. There were horses in the training depot and they had to be cleaned at 4am and then ridden until breakfast at 10am. Once out on a bush station there was not a horse in sight, and I never did get to ride a horse patrol in the bush. Because of the general misperception of the Congo mercenary, I was thought most suited for remote and dangerous stations. The Rhodesian Government declared independence from Britain during the six months I spent in the training depot. The war between the whites and the black nationalists had already started before that, and dragged on until Mugabe was eventually installed. I fought that war for a few months as a member of the paramilitary Police Support Unit and later as a member of the Police Anti-Terrorist Unit. My spell in the PATU spanned all of my service because of that mad six months in the Congo.

The white Rhodesians who could, ran far and hard away from the regime of Mugabe. Foreseeing what would happen in Rhodesia was not difficult and I came south. Now too old to run after 30 years in South Africa, the African jungle is stalking civilization and me again. Will the madness in Africa ever end?

Related titles published by Helion & Company and 30° South Publishers

Africa@War series – each paperback book in this series has
72pp, including 8pp colour photos/illustrations

*1: Operation Dingo. Rhodesian Raid
on Chimoio and Tembué, 1977*
J.R.T. Wood
ISBN 978-1-907677-36-6

*2: France in Centrafrique: From Bokassa and
Operation Barracuda to the days of EUFOR*
Peter Baxter
ISBN 978-1-907677-37-3

*3: Battle for Cassinga: South Africa's
Controversial Cross-Border Raid, Angola 1978*
Mike McWilliams
ISBN 978-1-907677-39-7

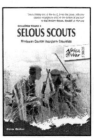

*4: Selous Scouts: Rhodesian Counter-
Insurgency Specialists*
Peter Baxter
ISBN 978-1-907677-38-0

Forthcoming titles

5: Zambezi Valley Insurgency. Early Rhodesian Bush War Operations
J.R.T. Wood
ISBN 978-1-907677-62-5

6: Congo Unravelled. Military Operations from Independence to the Mercenary Revolt 1960-68
Andrew Hudson
ISBN 978-1-907677-63-2

HELION & COMPANY
26 Willow Road, Solihull, West
Midlands B91 1UE, England
Telephone 0121 705 3393
Fax 0121 711 4075
Website: http://www.helion.co.uk

30° SOUTH PUBLISHERS (PTY) LTD
16 Ivy Road
Pinetown 3610
South Africa
email: info@30degreessouth.co.za
website: www.30degreessouth.co.za